A Social Psychological View of Education

THE PROFESSIONAL EDUCATION FOR TEACHERS SERIES

Under the Editorship of PAUL WOODRING

Editor of the Educational Supplement of the Saturday Review *and Distinguished Service Professor at Western Washington State College*

PUBLISHED TITLES

Introduction to American Education, Paul Woodring

Education and Democratic Ideals, Gordon C. Lee

Education in Western Culture, Robert Ulich

American Secondary Schools, Mauritz Johnson, Jr.

Teaching in a World of Change, Robert H. Anderson

Measuring Pupil Achievement and Aptitude, C. M. Lindvall

Learning, J. Charles Jones

A Social Psychological View of Education, Carl W. Backman and Paul F. Secord

A Social Psychological

View of Education

CARL W. BACKMAN and
PAUL F. SECORD

University of Nevada

Harcourt, Brace & World, Inc.
New York · Chicago · San Francisco · Atlanta

ACKNOWLEDGMENTS

We wish to express our gratitude to the University of Nevada for the sabbatical leave granted us for this project. For financial assistance on a closely related project involving critical reviews of research literature, we are much indebted to the United States Office of Education and to the Office of Economic Opportunity.

We would like to thank the following for permission to reprint material in this book:

ALLYN & BACON, INC.—For excerpts from C. R. Pace, "Differences in Campus Atmosphere" in W. W. Charters and N. L. Gage, eds., *Readings in the Social Psychology of Education*. Boston, Mass., Allyn & Bacon, 1963.

THE MACMILLAN COMPANY—For excerpt from Anne Anastasi, *Differential Psychology*, 3rd ed. New York, Macmillan, 1958 © The Macmillan Company, 1958.

QUADRANGLE BOOKS, INC.—For excerpt from Arthur L. Stinchcombe, *Rebellion in a High School*. Chicago, Ill., Quadrangle Books, 1964.

JOHN WILEY & SONS, INC., PUBLISHERS—For excerpts from George G. Stern, "Environments for Learning" in Nevitt Sanford, ed., *The American College*. New York, Wiley, 1962.

Editor's Foreword

Although universities find it convenient to divide scholarly and scientific knowledge into "academic disciplines," some of the most significant areas for research lie within the shadowy borderline regions between the conventional disciplines. In recent years a growing number of research scientists have given their attention to these areas, for which a hyphenated designation at first seemed necessary: astro-physics, bio-chemistry, and social-psychology. Gradually the hyphens were dropped and new disciplines emerged.

Social psychology is of particular significance to educators. The growing problems of urban education have given new urgency to the need for an understanding of the influence of social forces on individual development. If the teacher from a middle-class background is to deal effectively with children from other backgrounds—particularly those described as "disadvantaged"—it is essential for him to understand the influence of early family life, social patterns, and social class on aspiration, personality, and motivation. He should be aware of the growing evidence that the mental development of the child, including the measurable aspects of his intelligence, is substantially influenced by his preschool environment, which in turn reflects the social system and the culture in which it exists.

In recent years, and particularly during the past decade, a growing number of psychologists, sociologists, and anthropologists have explored the complex interrelationships among cultures, societies, and personalities, using a variety of sophisticated techniques. Illuminating discoveries have been made. But much of the new evidence has not yet found its way into the textbooks read by teachers—it appears in a wide range of scientific and scholarly journals that no teacher or student preparing himself for teaching can be expected to know at first hand.

The present volume is a careful distillation of the most significant research findings drawn from a wide variety of journals and presented here in an organized fashion and in readable language. At the end of each chapter the authors have included a section titled "Implications

v

for the Classroom" that makes clear to the teacher or prospective teacher just how the scientific evidence can be applied to his work in the classroom.

The paperback format makes it possible to combine this volume with others of the same series in a variety of ways, depending on the nature of the courses required of teachers in the various states and colleges. Where different course sequences are required, it can add an essential and often neglected ingredient to courses in educational psychology, child development, principles of education, social foundations, educational sociology, or introduction to the problems of education. It will be especially useful in refresher courses for teachers returning to summer school. However used, it will make teachers and prospective teachers better aware of the social forces that mold the personality of the child during his school years, and it will make the teachers' work more effective.

Professors Backman and Secord have contributed notably to the advancement of social psychology and particularly to the social psychology of education. Professor Backman is chairman of the Department of Sociology at the University of Nevada; Professor Secord is chairman of the Department of Psychology in the same institution. Individually and as a team they have contributed more than sixty titles to the professional and scholarly journals, and they are the authors of major textbooks and books of readings in social psychology and the social psychology of education. They are exceptionally well qualified to present the latest data on social psychology to teachers.

PAUL WOODRING

Contents

Introduction

This volume leads the reader to view the educational process through the eyes of a social psychologist. To do this he must become familiar with a number of basic concepts used by social psychologists. These concepts, like those of any science, help us focus upon and analyze phenomena in a fruitful manner. Of special interest to the social psychologist are uniformities of human behavior that characterize interaction between persons. These regularities of thought, feeling, and action constitute much of human behavior. They are described in terms of three general concepts—*social system, culture,* and *personality.*

SOCIAL SYSTEM

Recurrent patterns can be observed in every group of persons. In classroom after classroom of a college building, we can see one person, the teacher, standing at the front of the room talking to students, who are seated and listening with varying degrees of attentiveness, occasionally taking notes. In other parts of the building, other patterns of recurrent interactions are unfolding between deans and secretaries, between committee chairmen and committee members, and among students. These regular patterns of behavior are related to one another and are grouped conceptually by the social psychologist into what is called a *social system.*

Two sources of stability or regularity in such systems can be analytically distinguished—the *institutional* and the *subinstitutional.* Recurrent patterns of behavior in any group may be attributed, in varying proportion, to these two sources. Sometimes one source predominates, sometimes the other. The *institutional source* refers to *expectations* shared by the participants in interaction as to how each is supposed to behave. These rules of conduct, or *norms*, are maintained because, in varying degree, group members believe in their legitimacy and sanction their enforcement. Thus, both students and teachers usually agree that the teacher should maintain order in the classroom and should punish those who disrupt it. The basic unit of these systems is the *social role*, which comprises a *role category* and a set of associated *role expectations*. *Role category* refers to a category of persons occupying a given position in the system, *role expectations* to the expectations associated with that position. For example, the structure of the school may be described in terms of the social roles of teacher, pupil, superintendent, principal, school board member, and parent.

Institutional behavior is generally quite stable over time, even when persons who occupy positions within the structure leave and are replaced, because newcomers are exposed to the shared and stable role expectations of the institution and, further, because these expectations are compatible with the values of the society in which the institution is embedded.

The second source of regularity in human interaction, the *subinstitutional*, is identified in terms of certain "structures" that emerge directly from the interaction itself. As persons interact, they develop feelings of friendship or dislike for one another. More generally, they find that interaction with some persons is more rewarding and less costly than interaction with others. In any group we may identify subgroups of persons whose frequent associations with each other result in large part because each member interacts with those persons whose company he most enjoys at least cost to himself. We call such patterns the "liking" or *sociometric structure* of a group.

Attention to the direct consequences of interaction among persons also reveals group structures other than those characterized by friendship. The *power structure* is identified in terms of the relative amount of social influence wielded by each participant and emerges in part from the ability of each person to engage in satisfying interaction with other persons. This ability is a function of the resources he has for rewarding other participants and minimizing the psychological costs to them.

Again we must stress that such structures are shaped not only by subinstitutional sources but also by institutional sources. In a military organization, for example, power is derived largely from the role that is assigned to each member—from his military rank and function. But it does not derive solely from this institutional source. Personal characteristics such as persuasiveness, ability, and even likeability contribute to the degree of influence that one soldier may exert over another. At the opposite extreme, perhaps, is a child's play group, where the institutional contribution is minimal and where patterns of liking and of social power derive primarily from direct interaction. Here the personal resources and characteristics of the children, such as skill at play, friendliness or aggressiveness, considerateness, and other qualities, primarily determine the liking and power structures that are maintained. But although the personal resources of children are important in shaping liking patterns, institutional sources also contribute to liking. For example, the classroom seating pattern arranged by the teacher creates more frequent interactions among subgroups of children, providing the opportunity for the development of friendships. Psychological studies of friendships show that proximities of this kind are reflected in the liking or sociometric structures of groups.

Regular behavior patterns stemming largely from subinstitutional sources are less durable than those emerging from institutional sources. This is true because the structures underlying the interaction have emerged directly from the interaction itself. Unlike structures shaped by institutional sources, they have little support from sources other than the participants themselves. For example, friends may associate because they enjoy each other's company, and while brothers may also enjoy each other's company, they associate in part because this is expected of brothers. As we discuss various aspects of the educational process, we will offer further examples of the functioning of social systems.

CULTURE

Every human group shares systems of beliefs and knowledge that constitute the *culture* of the group. Of particular interest to the social psychologist are group values pertaining to behavior patterns and the systems of knowledge necessary to achieve and maintain these patterns. To illustrate, middle-class, suburban eighth-graders enrolled in a science class are apt to share the belief that good grades are important and that one way to get them is to turn in a good science project. This aspect of their subculture might lead to wide use of the resources of the local library. Children of similar age in an urban ghetto school may be indifferent to grades. They may believe that those who get good grades are just lucky. Students in this subculture might lack any knowledge about even the location of the nearest public library.

In this book we will analyze particularly those culture-wide values that pertain to educational achievement. There are interesting variations in such values from one subculture to another. As in the example above, these values vary with socioeconomic status and also with factors such as geographic area and ethnic group.

PERSONALITY

Whereas our focus thus far has been on the group, *personality* is a concept that applies to the individual. It refers to the unique combination of thoughts, feelings, and tendencies to act that distinguish a given individual from others. Though a variety of concepts have been used to organize knowledge about personality, social psychologists favor the concepts of *social motives* and *attitudes*. *Social motives* are individual tendencies to behave toward others in a characteristic fashion—to be aggressive, dependent, competitive, friendly, and so on. *Attitudes* are individual tendencies to think, feel, and act in a patterned fashion toward some object of experience—an aspect of one's physical environment, another person, a symbol, or even one's own behavior. Tendencies in regard to one's own behavior have been of particular interest to social psychologists because the cluster of feelings and impressions that a person has of himself, his *self* concept, are thought to greatly influence and be influenced by his relations with others. These three concepts—social motive, attitude, and self—direct our attention toward certain determinants of behavior in educational settings.

Two other concepts focus on *outcomes* of the educational process. The first is *socialization,* a process of interaction whereby a person's behavior is modified to conform to expectations held by members of a group to which he belongs. The second is *role allocation,* the process by which persons are selected for various role categories in social systems. Socialization and role allocation are particularly relevant to an understanding of education in contemporary society because the educational system plays a decisive part in both. Much of the culture of our society is systematically instilled into a child by his school, and many of the role categories that a child will later occupy are determined by how far he progresses in school. Our emphasis on the school, however, should not obscure the fact that a variety of other influences greatly affect behavior in the school situation. Family and peer group influences, as well as personality differences, mediate the effects of school experiences.

The organization of the book is as follows. Chapter One is based upon the revolutionary changes that have taken place in recent years in our thinking about child development and the nature of abilities. We no longer think of mental abilities as fixed endowments, nor do we think of development as an unfolding process governed solely by maturation. Current theory gives greater recognition to the nature of experience as a factor in child development. Thus, preschool socialization provides a suitable beginning point for Chapter One. In terms of their relation to the child's later achievement in school, we will discuss social class, parents as models, pressures for educational achievement, facilitating and interfering effects of the home environment, modes of child discipline, language training, and styles of interaction between parent and child.

Chapter Two focuses upon the individual student, reviewing studies that relate his abilities, attitudes, and personality to his educational achievement. The extent to which these are developed has much to do with whether the child gets off to a good start in school. Although these attributes are modifiable, they seem to become more stable with increasing age. This is not only due to intraperson processes, but is also a result of social forces in an individual's environment.

Chapter Three examines the school environment—the attitudes and aspirations of students and faculty, the curriculum pursued, the living groups, and friendship groups. The school is thought of as a miniature society, having its own culture, or climate, made up of a variety of identifiable subcultures that affect the behavior and performance of the student.

In Chapter Four, we examine in detail the role of the pupil from the beginning to the end of his formal education. During this period many choice points occur. The pupil meets forces which turn him in one direction or another, and in many instances his steps cannot easily be retraced. His choices often have an important connection to the role he will assume as an adult. Thus, we examine the factors in elementary education that produce high school dropouts and those that encourage entrance into college and, later, into graduate education.

Chapter Five looks closely at interaction between teacher and student and among students in the classroom. This is one of the most significant aspects of the school situation. It is in the classroom that friendships are formed and that intimate peer groups emerge; and it is the classroom teacher who most vividly represents the process of schooling itself. In this chapter we discuss control of student performance by the teacher and by the classroom group, as well as the conditions that create high or low motivation and satisfaction in regard to school work.

In Chapter Six the focus shifts specifically to the teacher. An application of contemporary role theory provides some insight into the determinants of his behavior and experiences.

Chapter One

Preschool Socialization
of the Student

In recent years, increasing importance has been attached to the preschool experiences of the child as determinants of his success in school. In part, this is due to revolutionary and still controversial changes in our thinking about child development that have occurred during the last two decades. No longer do we think of mental abilities as fixed endowments, nor do we think of development as an unfolding process governed overwhelmingly by maturation. We have found that the structure of the environment and the nature of experience profoundly affect the mental development of the child.[1] Careful analysis of growth in general educational achievement, reading comprehension, and vocabulary development has shown that about one-third of a person's total mental development takes place during the preschool period![2] This dramatically illustrates the importance of the preschool home environment for educational achievement. Chapter One focuses upon the factors within this home environment that appear to have the largest effect on mental development and performance. Before dealing specifically with the home environment, however, let us first discuss and evaluate the association between socioeconomic class and educational achievement.

EDUCATION AND SOCIAL CLASS

Social class is a sociological variable that has long been thought to be an important factor in educational achievement. The people in a community or a larger society may be conceptualized as fall-

---

1. J. McV. Hunt, *Intelligence and Experience* (New York: Ronald Press, 1961).
2. B. S. Bloom, *Stability and Change in Human Characteristics* (New York: Wiley, 1964).

ing into a number of classes, along a continuum from high to low. This continuum is multifaceted, representing both prestige and power and sometimes other components. Most commonly, occupation is used as a criterion for determining a person's social class, but income, education, residence, and family lineage are sometimes given weight. In smaller communities, the relative class status of each resident may be determined on the basis of subjective judgments by the people themselves.

Social class may affect education in several ways. First, attitudes toward education held by parents and children vary with social class. Second, the social-class membership of the child often determines where his family lives, and this in turn determines the public school that he attends. Whether a child has adequate means for financing his later education also depends upon his social-class membership. Finally, social class is important because the school system and its representatives, particularly the teacher and the counselor, reflect certain social-class values, and consequently they are apt to treat differently children from different social classes. We discuss attitudes toward education in this chapter and the other points in Chapter Four.

Studies determining the relation between social class and academic performance [3] demonstrate that the higher a person's social class, the higher is his level of academic performance. This positive relation holds for all educational levels but apparently does not hold for the upper social-class levels, particularly with respect to college performance. Some studies yield a negative relation for this portion of the social-class dimension—students at the bottom of the upper class perform better than students at the top. Two interpretations of this exception have been offered: First, upper-class students need only graduate to maintain their status, whereas middle-class students find college status-enhancing and strive for high performance.[4] Second, upper-class students come to college from private schools, where they experienced a more directed regimen,

3. D. E. Lavin, *The Prediction of Academic Performance* (New York: Russell Sage Foundation, 1965).

4. C. C. McArthur, "Personalities of Public and Private School Boys," *Harvard Educational Review*, Vol. 24 (1954), pp. 256–62; J. A. Davis and N. Frederiksen, "Public and Private School Graduates in College," *Journal of Teacher Education*, Vol. 6 (1955), pp. 18–22; J. A. Davis, "Differential College Achievement of Public vs. Private School Graduates," *Journal of Counseling Psychology*, Vol. 3 (1956), pp. 72–73.

and have more difficulty adjusting to the less-structured college environment.[5]

Since intelligence as measured by standardized tests is known to be associated with both educational achievement and social class,[6] it might be argued that the correlation between social class and educational achievement is an artificial result of the relation of each variable to intelligence. In two studies, when the effect of intelligence was removed by statistical means, the relation between social class and educational achievement dropped appreciably but not to zero.[7] This result means that the relation between social class and performance in school is in part due to the systematic association between intelligence and social class. But it also means that school performance is associated with other aspects of social class that have nothing to do with intelligence. Later in this chapter we shall identify these other factors.

Educational values and their relation to occupational goals account in part for the relation between social class and educational achievement. Numerous studies agree in suggesting that, in a general and abstract sense, education is universally valued among all social classes. For example, in a survey of attitudes of inhabitants of New York City's Lower East Side, a slum area for generations, about 95 percent of the respondents stated that "a good education is essential to getting ahead." [8] Furthermore, when asked what came to mind when they thought of a "good life" for children, more than half mentioned education. Education was mentioned by as many lower-class persons as middle-class persons (there were no upper-class persons in the sample). An extensive survey sponsored by the United States Office of Education similarly found only slight differences in educational aspirations among students of varying social backgrounds.[9]

---

5. Lavin, *op. cit.*
6. *Ibid.*
7. W. H. Friedhoff, "Relationships Among Various Measures of Socioeconomic Status, Social Class Identification, Intelligence, and School Achievement," *Dissertation Abstracts,* Vol. 15 (1955), p. 2098; L. M. Knief and J. B. Stroud, "Intercorrelations Among Various Intelligence, Achievement, and Social-Class Scores," *Journal of Educational Psychology,* Vol. 50 (1959), pp. 117–20.
8. R. A. Cloward and J. A. Jones, "Social Class: Educational Attitudes and Participation," in A. H. Passow, ed., *Education in Depressed Areas* (New York: Teachers College Press, Columbia University, 1963), pp. 190–216.
9. J. S. Coleman, E. Q. Campbell, C. J. Hobson, *et al., Equality of Educational Opportunity* (Washington, D.C.: U.S. Office of Education, 1966).

On the other hand, varying answers were reported to this question asked of a national sample: "About how much schooling do you think most young men need these days to get along well in the world?" [10] The percentage of those recommending a college education differed markedly by class, as follows: among the wealthy and prosperous, 74 percent; among the middle class, 63 percent; and among the lower class, only 42 percent. While lower-class persons value education in a general sense highly, they also realize that, for them, it is less apt to be a means to obtaining a desirable job. Respondents in another sample reacted similarly to those in the national sample. Lower-class persons less frequently felt that a good education was essential to getting ahead.[11] This difference occurs because, in general, lower-class individuals have lower occupational goals. This in turn represents a somewhat realistic perception of inequalities in job opportunities. Particularly where a lower-class person also belongs to a disadvantaged ethnic group, for example, if he is a Negro, he will have a difficult time finding employment opportunities equal to those found by middle-class persons who have a comparable education and who do not belong to a disadvantaged ethnic group. Negro youths with college training are often employed in semi-skilled and lower white-collar positions because higher level jobs are not available to them in sufficient numbers. We may conclude that persons whose occupational goals are more limited are less apt to view educational achievement as necessary for occupational success. Further, lower-class parents are less likely to provide vigorous support for school activities and are less apt to encourage their children to stay in school beyond the required minimum number of years.

Before we conclude, however, that the varying parental and student aspirations in different social classes partly account for differences in academic achievement, we must first dispose of a counterargument. Just as educational achievement is associated with intelligence, so are educational aspirations. Thus, it might be argued that the correlation between social class and educational aspiration is simply an artificial result of the association of each variable with intelligence. This argument has been refuted, however, by a study of high school seniors which showed social class

10. Herbert Hyman, *Political Socialization* (New York: Macmillan, 1959).
11. Cloward and Jones, *op. cit.*

and educational aspiration to be directly associated *even among individuals approximately equal in intelligence.*[12]

A number of other factors impoverish the education of lower-class children.[13] Teachers are reluctant to teach in slum-area schools and transfer out of such schools at a more rapid rate. The vacancies created are often filled by newly graduated, inexperienced teachers, who have the least bargaining power in seeking a position.[14] Naturally they are apt to be less skilled and less effective teachers. In addition, in such schools, a greater proportion of classroom and school activity involves organizational and disciplinary matters, reducing the amount of time devoted to instruction. One study of slum-area schools found that 50 to 80 percent of the day was spent in disciplinary or organizational details and only 30 to 50 percent in actual instruction.[15]

In certain ways, the influence of social class on educational achievement has been overemphasized in the older educational literature.[16] While social class has some importance in the early school years, in later years cross-class socialization usually occurs. Most high schools develop common norms and behavior patterns that cut across class lines. This gives the lower-class high school child an opportunity to acquire some of the values and attitudes of social classes other than his own. Nevertheless, it must be kept in mind that a poor start in the preschool period and in the early grades, where social class may well have an effect, is likely to have enduring consequences for later performance.

Recent findings in the United States and Britain have shown that graded primaries produce even further differences among the segregated groups. Social class, which is often responsible for the quality of a child's start in the graded primary school, takes on still greater importance in this light. The educational experiences of chil-

---

12. W. H. Sewell, A. O. Haller, and M. A. Straus, "Social Status and Educational and Occupational Aspiration," *American Sociological Review*, Vol. 22 (1957), pp. 67–73.
13. Cloward and Jones, *op. cit.*
14. H. S. Becker, "The Career of the Chicago Public School Teacher," *American Sociological Review*, Vol. 17 (1952), pp. 470–76.
15. M. P. Deutsch, "Minority-Group and Class Status as Related to Social and Personality Factors in Scholastic Achievement," Monograph No. 2 (Society for Applied Anthropology, 1960).
16. W. B. Brookover and D. Gottlieb, "Social Class and Education," in W. W. Charters, Jr., and N. L. Gage, eds., *Readings in the Social Psychology of Education* (Boston: Allyn and Bacon, 1963), pp. 3–11.

dren in low-ability groups cause them to learn at a slower rate, while high-ability groups are stimulated to learn at a more rapid rate. With each year, the gap between low-ability and high-ability children widens. This tendency of early behavior patterns to persist in later years is discussed further in Chapter Two; the social forces affecting the child's pattern of movement through various educational levels and grades are described in Chapter Four.

A widely recognized limitation of the social-class dimension is that it represents only grossly several specific variables—such factors as the attitudes of the family toward education, its educational and occupational aspirations, the intellectual environment it provides, the stress it places on striving to achieve success, and the forms of discipline and control used by the parents. These factors do vary roughly with social class, but they also vary considerably *within* class levels. A family at a particular social-class level will rarely correspond in all dimensions to its social-class position. Thus, current research tends to go beyond social class and to examine relations between educational achievement and each of the specific variables associated with social class. If relations between these specific family variables and educational achievement can be determined, we will have a more precise understanding of the school performance of any particular child and also a better idea of what kinds of social action might improve the educational system. We attempt this type of analysis in the following discussion. We will also note from time to time the extent to which these specific factors do vary with social class.

We have already noted that, as we move from lower to higher social strata, an increasing proportion of persons see education as preparation for a desirable occupation. Families also vary *within* a social class in the stress they place on education as a means to occupational success. For instance, among a group of 202 lower-class, Negro mothers with children in nursery school or kindergarten, those with less education and more children envisioned fewer years of education for their children and had lower occupational aspirations for them. They more frequently perceived a technical education as adequate and less often saw hard work and ambition as a means to success.[17]

17. R. R. Bell, "Variation Among Lower-Class Negro Mothers Related to Aspirations for Their Children," paper read at American Psychological Association, Los Angeles, September 1964.

FAMILY AND EDUCATIONAL ACHIEVEMENT

Textbooks on social psychology discuss certain general processes that operate in the family situation to shape the attitudes and behavior of the child.[18] We review them briefly here but will give more attention to family variables that relate directly to success or failure in school.

Parents and older siblings serve as *models* for behavior patterns appropriate to the cultural group to which they belong. If they are members of the middle class, for example, their behavior is apt to exemplify the value of material possessions and the importance of competing for wealth and position. Parents also *sanction* culturally approved behavior. When a child's behavior deviates too radically from accepted patterns he may be punished. Similarly, he is rewarded when he adopts acceptable patterns of behavior. Such sanctions are used, for example, to teach the child proper table manners.

In our own modern, highly developed society, values and behavior patterns differ from one subgroup to another. They vary by social class, by rural or urban residence, and by geographical regions of the United States. Thus, each family represents the cultural values and behavior patterns of its subculture. While some cultural elements are common to almost every family, others are specific to particular subcultures.

In addition to providing models for and reinforcing appropriate behaviors and values, the family mediates culture by filtering and interpreting the values and behaviors of subgroups differing from its own. In our highly mobile society, the child is frequently exposed to such groups, not only in actual contacts but especially through television and movies. Although this exposure broadens his experience to some extent, the family limits this broadening by interpreting these outside experiences for the child in ways which reinforce the culture patterns of its own subgroup. For example, suppose that parents are strongly prejudiced against a particular minority group. Then communications reaching the child in the home that put members of this group in a favorable light are apt to be discredited or given a distorted interpretation.

18. P. F. Secord and C. W. Backman, *Social Psychology* (New York: McGraw-Hill, 1964).

In recent years interest in the impact of various subcultures on the educational process has greatly intensified. Most notably, the increasing urbanization of our society, with its attendant increases in the size and number of underprivileged urban groups, has made the problem of educating the deprived child a dominant one. Ambitious research programs studying the impact of subcultures on the educational process are now under way and, ultimately, should greatly increase our knowledge. A review of our present knowledge is useful, however, in providing a tentative basis for action and for further research. We will first consider the impact of family socialization practices on the initial adjustment of the child to the school situation and, in later chapters, discuss how the educational process is affected by the peer group and by the culture of the school.

Unfortunately, much research attempting to relate the home environment of the child to his school achievements fails to yield unimpeachable conclusions, partly because of its newness and partly because of the failure of investigators to apply well-known experimental and statistical controls in their work. The most common problem is that of demonstrating that an antecedent variable or condition is *causally* related to educational achievement. This problem arises because, by itself, the demonstration of an association between two variables in a nonlaboratory setting does not imply a cause-effect relation. Often the association between two variables may be a function of the correlation of each with a third variable. An example may clarify this point.

Suppose that one wished to discover whether an intellectually stimulating environment in the home produced a higher level of educational achievement. Quantitative data might be obtained on such items as the number of books and "quality" magazines in the home, the presence of one or more encyclopedias, and the extent of discussion between adults and children that could be characterized as intellectual. Such data could be correlated with educational achievement, testing the hypothesis that a positive association exists between the intellectual level of the home environment and achievement in school. Unfortunately, even if a very high association were found, this information by itself would not demonstrate that the home environment *determines* the level of educational achievement. Various noncausal explanations of this correlation may readily be imagined. Two examples are:

1. Families with larger incomes undoubtedly can afford to purchase a larger number of books and have more space for them in their homes. Such families also live in more expensive residential areas, where the schools are better supported financially and thus are more able to operate effectively in educating children from these families.

2. We may assume that educational achievement is at least in part accounted for by inherited characteristics that relate to intelligent behavior. (This viewpoint is currently under vigorous attack but has not yet been convincingly refuted.) Another explanation then suggests itself for the obtained association between the intellectual level of the home and educational achievement—simply that intelligent parents buy more books and also, for genetic reasons, have children who are more intelligent and who consequently perform well in school.

Methods of analysis are available for ruling out alternative interpretations that would otherwise make it extremely difficult to draw convincing conclusions from the findings of such research,[19] but these methods have seldom been used in educational research. A simple and commonly used procedure is to make comparisons within subgroups *equated* on the unwanted variable or variables. For example, if the positive correlation between the intellectual level of the home environment and educational achievement drops to zero when only those children whose parents perform similarly on an intelligence test are considered, the original correlation may be considered spurious. If, on the other hand, the positive association is not diminished by such an analysis, the intellectual environment of the home has clearly been shown to affect achievement independently of the parents' intelligence. One difficulty with this method is that each of many plausible alternate explanations must be eliminated before much confidence may be placed in the obtained correlation. Another problem is that large numbers of persons must be included in the sample.

Many characteristics of the family affect the educational achieve-

---

19. P. Kendall and P. F. Lazarsfeld, "Problems of Survey Analysis," in R. K. Merton and P. F. Lazarsfeld, eds., *Continuities in Social Research: Studies in the Scope and Method of "The American Soldier"* (New York: Macmillan, 1950), pp. 136–47; C. W. Backman and P. F. Secord, eds., *Problems in Social Psychology: Selected Readings* (New York: McGraw-Hill, 1966), pp. 27–34.

ment of children. Among these are the value and meaning the family attaches to education, the pressures parents create toward achievement, the extent to which the home environment stimulates intellectual development, the language model provided by adults in the family, the forms of discipline and control used by parents, the academic guidance parents provide, and the extent to which the home situation facilitates desirable work habits.

Before proceeding further, there may be merit in describing at least briefly some important theoretical notions concerning the development of the child's ability to use *concepts*. As part of a sophisticated theory, Harvey, Hunt, and Schroder have proposed that the use of concepts varies from the *concrete* to the *abstract*.[20] In a favorable life situation, children are thought to progress through four stages, from an initial stage where concepts are concrete to a final stage where they are abstract. In many instances, however, the behavior of socializing agents interferes with progression to the next stage or fixes conceptual development at one of the earlier stages.

At the initial stage, which is the most concrete, evaluations of things or events are good or bad, black or white. Action is guided by strong dependency on authority. Ambiguous situations are disturbing and require resolution even at the risk of oversimplification. Children experience difficulty in seeing alternate routes to the same goal. The capacity to "act as if," to assume the role of another person, or to act in terms of a hypothetical situation has not been developed. The self is less well defined and less apt to be perceived as a causal agent in behavior sequences. Abstractness, on the other hand, is represented by the opposite of these characteristics.

The following are the four stages of this developmental sequence:

STAGE 1. Concrete conceptual functioning results from training conditions in which the parent exercises complete or near-complete control over the child. The parent sets a rather rigidly prescribed path for the child to tread without explaining the reasons and values associated with this particular behavior. A child in this stage may be expected to be strongly dependent upon authority, to re-

---

20. O. J. Harvey, D. E. Hunt, and H. M. Schroder, *Conceptual Systems and Personality Organization* (New York: Wiley, 1961).

quire highly structured situations, and to approach problems in a narrow, stereotyped fashion.

STAGE II. Functioning here is still largely concrete, but the parent is more unpredictable and capricious in his demands and in his administration of rewards and punishments. Clear routes to the attainment of rewards are not perceived. The child rebels against external authority and is negativistic. Self may be somewhat better differentiated because of the need to rely on his own resources.

STAGE III. Rules and external authority are less influential in this stage. The behavior of the child is determined by a reciprocal relation between himself and his parents. He develops some sensitivity to the desires of his parents and adapts to them, just as they adapt to his needs, and this contributes to his understanding of self. Frequently, however, this reciprocal relation is not balanced, and either the parents' or the child's needs are the center of focus. Stress on parental needs results in overdependency, and excess emphasis on the child's needs in parental overprotection. Overdependency is associated with a passive approach to learning and with a lack of creativity and originality, while overprotectiveness deprives the child of practice in coping with problems.

STAGE IV. Both parent and child have a task orientation to situations. This occurs because the child has gained rewards through his own exploration rather than by matching his behavior to criteria set by the parent. His evaluation of self is positive and is based upon successful achievement. Thus, he has an open-minded approach to problem-solving and to accepting new ideas.

Although the foregoing brief treatment of this theory cannot possibly do it justice, these main outlines of the concreteness-abstractness dimension are helpful in organizing thinking on our main problem: the effects of family socialization processes on educational achievement.

The extent to which parents directly pressure their children toward achievement in school and toward other valued achievements is often thought to be an important determinant of the child's success in school. Studies on this point are conflicting, however. Some studies find a direct association between the amount of pressure toward achievement exerted by parents and the amount of actual achievement by the child. Others find zero relationships, and still others find negative relationships.

For example, a recent investigation measuring achievement pressure used intensive interviews with 60 families having children in the fifth grade. Questions were asked about parental aspirations for the education of the child, the parent's own aspirations, parental interest in academic activities, direct parental pressure for achievement in school, parental rewards for educational achievement, knowledge of the educational progress of their children, and preparation and planning for the attainment of educational goals.[21] An overall measure of this parental achievement orientation correlated very highly with the child's achievement in school, higher than in most studies. But this high association is not to be interpreted as representing the extent to which parental pressure for achievement *causes* a child to perform well in school. The parental achievement measure included some items that were actually a function of the child's progress in school. For example, one question pertained to the parents' knowledge of their children's progress. But when children do outstandingly well in school, or do very poorly, parents may become especially aware of this fact. The exceptional performance is thus antecedent to the parents' knowledge rather than the other way around.

Another study of 40 early-grade school children and their parents found no relation between the value the fathers and mothers placed upon their children's intellectual performance and the children's observed performance. Furthermore, encouragement of and participation in intellectual activities with the child by the parent was negatively associated with the children's school performance.[22]

A recent study suggests that only certain types of pressures are related to educational ambitions.[23] Two groups were assembled, each containing 50 working-class families. Sons in one group had decided to attend college upon graduation; sons in the other had not. The two groups of boys were matched on intelligence and on community residence. Although parental planning and encouragement for their sons' future was much more prevalent in the college-

21. R. H. Dave, "The Identification and Measurement of Environmental-Process Variables That Are Related to Educational Achievement," unpublished doctoral dissertation, University of Chicago, 1963.
22. V. J. Crandall, R. Dewey, W. Katkovsky, and A. Preston, "Parents' Attitudes and Behaviors and Grade School Children's Academic Achievements," *Journal of Genetic Psychology*, Vol. 104 (1964), pp. 53–66.
23. E. G. Cohen, "Parental Factors in Educational Mobility," *Sociology of Education*, Vol. 38 (1965), pp. 404–25.

bound group, there was little difference between groups in more direct, immediate parental pressures, such as might be expected in response to poor grade reports. At this stage of knowledge, we may conclude that directly encouraging children to succeed in school does not necessarily improve their performance—a conclusion that many parents have ruefully arrived at through their own experience.

One reason why such studies do not yield consistent results is that parents' attitudes toward their children's school achievements must also be considered in combination with the characteristic means they use to control and train their children. Very probably, identical parental attitudes toward education have different effects depending upon the disciplinary techniques they use, although there is little evidence for this. Many studies have shown that the types of discipline themselves are related to children's school achievements, although the results of the researchers have not always been consistent. In early studies, positive parental attitudes toward the child (such as high interest in the child, closeness to him, understanding and approval of him) were associated with achievement in high school.[24] However, various methodological inadequacies of these investigations undermine confidence in this initial conclusion. More recent studies agree in demonstrating that *negative* parental behaviors (such as rejection, coerciveness, overprotection) relate to high achievement. The research also suggests that somewhat different behavior on the part of the father and the mother toward boys and toward girls produces optimum academic achievement. Training the child to be independent at an early age, initially thought to be positively related to achievement, in a more recent study appears to be negatively associated.[25] Mothers who accept and foster *dependence* have children who do better in school.

One explanation of these conflicting results may be that the relation between parental stress on academic achievement and the child's actual progress in school is curvilinear. Too little or too much stress may lower academic achievement; a moderate amount may yield optimum performance. A parent who is too critical and demanding and too sparing of praise and support can produce dis-

---

24. V. J. Crandall, "Achievement," in H. W. Stevenson, ed., *Child Psychology: The Sixty-second Yearbook of the National Society for the Study of Education, Part I* (Chicago: University of Chicago Press, 1963), pp. 416–59.
25. J. E. Chance, "Independence Training and First Graders' Achievement," *Journal of Consulting Psychology*, Vol. 25 (1961), pp. 149–54.

couragement and negative attitudes toward school, while one who is indiscriminately supportive may fail to motivate his child toward achievement. Clinical studies relate the school failure of some children to overpowering parental ambitions and of others to parental indifference. Since various investigations use different measures of parental attitudes toward achievement, it is difficult to assess whether they are at the optimum point. Another study notes that parental exhortations and standards of achievement are accepted only when the child identifies strongly with his parents.[26] This condition is fostered by a warm nurturant relation between parent and child.

The limitations of studies using a cross-sectional design should also be noted. If information on parent and child behavior is collected at only one point in time, and they are found not to be related, it is still possible that parental behavior might produce delayed effects not measured by the investigation. A good example of this "sleeper effect" has been noted in a study of 89 children and their parents carried on over a period of 30 years.[27] One measure obtained at various age periods was the mother's interest in accelerating the physical and mental development of her child. The child's achievement at adulthood was found to be more highly correlated with the mother's efforts at acceleration occurring during the first three years of life than with her efforts at any of the later age periods. One possible interpretation of this rather surprising result is that the mother's initial attitude toward her infant, before his distinctive personality characteristics emerge, is a more adequate index of her basic child-rearing attitudes. Later, a mother's reactions to her child are markedly affected by his behavior toward her.

The developmental theory of Harvey, Hunt, and Schroder suggests two other points.[28] One is that the different stages of development undoubtedly call for different types of parental behavior. Poorly timed use of wrong socialization practices at a particular age may have undesirable effects, which can be assessed only through longitudinal studies. The second point is that some knowledge of the school situation is essential. A child whose family produces in him a relatively concrete orientation, with heavy dependence on authority

26. M. Argyle and W. P. Robinson, "Two Origins of Achievement Motivation," *British Journal of Social and Clinical Psychology*, Vol. 1 (1962), pp. 107–20.
27. J. Kagan and H. A. Moss, *Birth to Maturity: A Study in Psychological Development* (New York: Wiley, 1962).
28. Harvey, Hunt, and Schroder, *op. cit.*

and a stereotyped approach to problem-solving, may do well under an authoritarian teacher who makes use of drill and rote learning. The opposite would be the case for a child who has acquired a more abstract style of conceptualization, stressing alternate approaches to problem-solving and independence in learning.

Differences in the way mothers teach their children to deal with the school system may have important consequences for learning.[29] Mothers may be characterized as having either a *status* orientation or a *person* orientation. The status-oriented mother stresses the difference in status and power between the teacher and child and encourages compliance and docility in adjusting to the classroom situation. In contrast, the person-oriented mother is less apt to view the school as a remote, implacable authority and consequently is less concerned with obedience. She attempts to acquaint her children with alternative types of behavior and the consequences of each, as well as with the purposes of various rules and behaviors. Status orientation is thought to produce passive and docile behavior, and person orientation, to produce active, inquiring behavior. In general, lower-class mothers tend to be status-oriented, and middle-class mothers tend to be person-oriented. These concepts closely resemble the dimension called concreteness-abstractness, with the status-oriented mother tending to produce a concrete conceptual system in the child, and the person-oriented mother a more abstract system.

Another aspect of the home that may relate to educational achievement is the suitability of the home environment for the development of *cognitive skills*. The home environment in depressed urban areas is especially deficient in this respect.[30] Living space is small; the number of people occupying a given space is large. The noise level is apt to be high, with continual strains resulting from the conflicting needs of individuals occupying a small space. Thus, privacy and freedom from distraction are rare. Magazines, books, toys, puzzles, pictures, furniture, and similar objects are relatively scarce in the home, creating a somewhat impoverished visual environment.

---

29. R. D. Hess, "Maternal Teaching Styles and the Socialization of Educability," paper read at American Psychological Association, Los Angeles, September 1964.

30. M. P. Deutsch, "The Disadvantaged Child and the Learning Process: Some Social Psychological and Developmental Considerations," in A. H. Passow, *op. cit.*

While it is logical to assume that such environments are less conducive to cognitive growth, it is hard to prove that this is the case. Experimental animals raised in severely restricted environments frequently perform poorly at adulthood and exhibit emotional disturbances, but control animals given brief daily experience in normal environments, although otherwise restricted, perform normally as adults. Thus, a minimum amount of daily exposure to a more normal environment may be all that is necessary to counteract the conditions which characterize the life of the child in the slum. Of course, generalization from animal studies on this issue is hazardous, for the child's learning during the preschool period is enormously complex compared to that of the rat or chimpanzee.

Another variable is the sheer amount of interaction between parent and child. Interaction is greatly reduced in many depressed-area homes.[31] Often the home has no father, and the mother must fill two roles, serving as both breadwinner and responsible caretaker for the family. Such families often have many children, a condition which also reduces interaction between the parent and each individual child. This reduced interaction produces, in effect, less intellectual stimulation of the child. Some support for this view is found in a report demonstrating that children from fatherless homes have significantly lower intelligence-test scores by the time they get to the fifth grade.[32] The interaction hypothesis is further supported by several other findings. First, within a social-class level, the larger the family, the lower is the intelligence-test performance of the children.[33] Second, the eldest child in a family tends to have a higher IQ—he had the greatest opportunity to interact with parents before the birth of his siblings.[34] Third, twins have lower IQ's than "only children." [35] Fourth, the IQ of children well spaced in age within

---

31. *Ibid.*

32. M. P. Deutsch and B. Brown, "Social Influences in Negro-white Intelligence Differences," *Journal of Social Issues*, Vol. 20, No. 2 (1964), pp. 24–35.

33. *Scottish Mental Survey*, see J. W. B. Douglas and J. M. Bloomfield, *Children Under Five* (London: MacGibbon & Kee, 1958); *Scottish Mental Survey*, see J. W. B. Douglas, *The Home and the School* (London: MacGibbon & Kee, 1964).

34. J. P. Lees and A. H. Stewart, "Family and Sibship Position and Scholastic Ability," *Sociological Review* (July, December 1957).

35. R. Gille *et al.*, "Le Niveau intellectuel des enfants d'âge scolaire: la détermination des aptitudes; l'influence des facteurs constitutionnels, familiaux, et sociaux," cited in J. McV. Hunt, *op. cit.*; J. D. Nisbet, *Family Environment: A Direct Effect of Family Size on Intelligence* (London: Cassell, 1963).

the family is higher than the IQ of children more closely spaced.[36] All this evidence suggests that a lower volume of interaction between parent and child results in lowered intellectual performance.

Perhaps the most important aspect of this interaction, for intellectual growth, is the verbal communication that takes place. Interaction among humans is largely verbal. School learning in particular is heavily dependent upon language skills. The interaction hypothesis just discussed suggests that the lower-class child is especially apt to be retarded in verbal development. Supporting this is the finding that the negative correlation between IQ and family size is greater for verbal than for nonverbal intelligence. Several other studies indicate that, among British working-class families, verbal intelligence is markedly depressed compared to nonverbal intelligence.[37]

Along similar lines, it has been argued that language differences among the social classes are not simply a matter of vocabulary or more proper use of grammar but rather that middle- and working-class families each use different *modes* of speech appropriate to their life situations. These modes have been defined as the *restricted code* and the *elaborated code*.[38] In terms of content, the *restricted code* pertains to easily predictable, ritualistic modes of communication such as would occur in interactions that are strongly governed by clearly understood rules. Examples are superficial exchanges between strangers who have just met and a mother telling her child bedtime stories that both know by heart. In terms of structure, the restricted code is relatively simple, with little expression of intent. This stems from a social relation of an inclusive kind, based upon a common, extensive set of closely shared identifications and expectations self-consciously held by the members. Individual feelings are conveyed primarily through nonverbal means. Meanings are likely to be concrete, descriptive, or narrative, not analytical or

---

36. L. Tabah and J. Sutter, "Le Niveau intellectuel des enfants d'une même famille," cited in J. McV. Hunt, *op. cit.*

37. Basil Bernstein, "Some Sociological Determinants of Perception: An Enquiry into Sub-cultural Differences," *British Journal of Sociology*, Vol. 9 (1958), pp. 159–67; "Language and Social Class," *British Journal of Sociology*, Vol. 11 (1960), pp. 271–76; Elizabeth Venables, in *Fifteen to Eighteen*, Vol. 1, Report of the Central Advisory Council for Education, Ministry of Education (London: Her Majesty's Stationery Office, 1959).

38. Basil Bernstein, "A Sociolinguistic Approach to Social Learning," in J. Gould, ed., *Social Science Survey* (London: Pelican, 1965).

abstract. The prototype of a restricted code is illustrated in the jargon used by adolescent peer groups, prison units, and military units.

Speech in an *elaborated code* is tailored more precisely to specific situations; the speaker is apt to modify his speech to fit the special conditions and attributes of the listener. There is greater sensitivity to nuances and differences of meaning; the intentions of both speaker and listener are taken into account.

These concepts fit fairly well the concreteness-abstractness dimension previously mentioned. In fact, this emphasis on language has in common with the developmental theory a central stress on the formation of different conceptual systems.

Although middle-class children use both restricted and elaborated modes of communication, depending upon their appropriateness to the situation, most lower-class children know only the restricted mode. Since the school situation requires an elaborated code of communication, the lower-class child may have difficulties in the classroom. He is apt to have little motivation to extend his vocabulary and to use words in new ways because he does not understand the mode of communication required. Although the restricted mode is compatible with rote learning and drill, it creates difficulties in generalizing from the specific content learned and in grasping the abstract principles typical of school learning.[39]

Using the concept of restricted and elaborated codes, researchers studied the use of language by 163 Negro mothers and their four-year-old children from 4 social-class levels.[40] They conducted intensive interviews with the mothers at home and set up several mother-child testing situations at the University of Chicago. The study showed that when the mother used a restricted mode of communication, the child was less apt to weigh reflectively alternative modes of action and to attend to the individual characteristics of a situation. Those mothers who used an elaborated code produced in their children a cognitive style more amenable to problem-solving behavior. As in England, the elaborated code was more typical of higher class levels, and the restricted code, of lower class levels.

39. Basil Bernstein, "Social Structure, Language and Learning," *Educational Research*, Vol. III (1961).
40. R. D. Hess and V. C. Shipman, "Early Experience and the Socialization of Cognitive Modes in Children," *Child Development*, Vol. 36 (1965), pp. 869–86.

Variation from class to class in these communication modes was greater than would be expected on the basis of the obtained intelligence-test differences.

Another study involved a core sample of 292 Negro and white children from the middle and lower classes. The first and fifth grades were represented. Over 100 variables concerned with home background, language functioning, conceptual behavior, intelligence-test performance, reading, general orientation, self concepts, and related factors were assessed by testing and other techniques.[41] Three language components are especially important in test performance. The first is *labeling*, which involves learning coded designations for objects and events in the child's environment, such as when the child learns the word "spoon" for the appropriate utensil. Second is *relating*, which involves fitting together the names of objects with descriptive modifiers into meaningful wholes, as in learning "small spoon" and "large spoon." Third is *categorizing*, which involves grouping objects or events into schemes on the basis of some conceptual framework, such as learning that a group of children running about in a certain fashion are "playing tag." These ideas appear to range from concreteness to abstractness in the sense discussed earlier.

Clear differences in performances on the tests related to these language components were found at the first-grade level between lower-class and middle-class children. Some racial differences were also found, but most of these were simultaneously associated with social-class differences. At the fifth-grade level, similar differences in performance were found, except that minority-group status was associated with deficiency in language skills to a greater extent than at the first-grade level. This supports the "cumulative deficit" hypothesis: when four years of school experience are added to a poor home environment and minority-group status, children are increasingly disadvantaged in language skills and intellectual tasks.

In conclusion, we should note several general criticisms of the research in this area. One is that too many studies are cross-sectional, limited to a single point in time, and too few are longitudinal, studying the same children over a period of years. It seems probable that a persistent but sensible and positive parental attitude toward

---

41. M. P. Deutsch, "The Role of Social Class in Language Development and Cognition," *American Journal of Orthopsychiatry*, Vol. 35 (1965), pp. 78–88.

achievement, generalized and stable over the entire developmental period, would correlate substantially with achievement, though at any given stage the correlation could be zero or even negative. In addition, different stages of development undoubtedly call for somewhat different types of parental behavior.

Second, a particular mode of child-rearing may facilitate academic performance at one age, but at another the same parental behavior might be detrimental to academic performance. Thus, differences among various studies might be easier to reconcile if we had knowledge of the relation at successive ages. A third point is that some familiarity with the school situation is essential if academic achievement is to be predicted from knowledge of the home situation. Child-rearing practices cannot be considered in isolation from the school situation. Analysis of what happens in the classroom in terms of the relation between teacher and pupil is necessary, and these interactions must be *compared* with what occurs at home between parent and child. For example, in the research just discussed on interpersonal styles,[42] it seems to be assumed that status-oriented interaction between mother and child will somehow be incompatible with the school situation while person-oriented interaction between mother and child will be compatible. But how is this known without careful study of the school situation? Anyone familiar with the atmosphere in public schools is aware of the considerable amount of control and discipline exerted in the school and classroom and of the authority-oriented nature of much interaction. In view of this, perhaps interaction between mother and child that is oriented in terms of status and authority would be more compatible with the school situation than a person-oriented style of interaction. Even more likely is the possibility that some midpoint between the two extremes of status-oriented interaction and person-oriented interaction would best prepare the child for competent performance in school.

If this is so, it means that extensive studies must be undertaken to discover the relative frequency of different styles of interaction between parent and child on one hand, and teacher and pupil on the other. Only after the research has been done in both settings can the effects of the home on the school be understood.

---

42. Hess, *op. cit.*

Implications for the Classroom

An understanding of the ideas presented in this chapter should alert the teacher to factors in the home that are apt to affect the performance of the children he teaches. The child from an impoverished home has a scanty fund of basic knowledge and insufficiently developed skills for adequate performance in the first grade. This does not mean that he is "stupid," in the inherent sense of the word, but only that he has not had sufficient informal training at home in the kinds of skills needed in school. A special effort to correct these deficiencies is called for. In particular, such a child needs training in language skills. Much ingenuity is required to interest him in school activities, which are more foreign to him than to a child from a middle- or an upper-class home.

Another partial solution to the problem of inadequate home environments is to extend the school day to include supervised periods for individual study and assigned work—since homework is apt to be done poorly or not at all where home conditions are inadequate.

Parents from deprived-area homes are less interested in and less involved in their child's education. Schools in such areas might engage in vigorous community programs in an attempt to involve parents in educational activities. The school should become a center for all sorts of community activities, in the hope that participants would then develop more interest in its primary function of education. At a more individual level, frequent conferences between parents and teachers might be held concerning the progress of their children. In deprived areas, teachers or other school representatives might make regular visits to the homes of parents who cannot otherwise be reached.

To accomplish the remedial activities suggested and to engage in community action, schools having a large proportion of children from deprived homes need to have fewer students per teacher, and they need experienced, highly skilled teachers. This is the opposite of the prevailing situation. Such schools are typically overcrowded and have the most poorly trained, least experienced teachers (see Chapter Four).

Chapter Two

The Individual Student:
Abilities and Personality

The preceding chapter focused primarily on the home environment of the child and its effect on his educational achievement. Little has been said so far about factors within the individual that are relatively stable when in a supportive environment, and that affect his academic performance. These include *intelligence, abilities, attitudes, interests,* and *personality variables* such as need for achievement, anxiety, introversion, and conceptions of self. The present chapter examines these variables in relation to educational achievement.

INTELLIGENCE, ABILITY,
AND EDUCATIONAL ACHIEVEMENT

Treatment of the great mass of research material pertaining to abilities and aptitudes and their relation to educational achievement is beyond the scope of this book. Such material is ordinarily given a central place in conventional educational psychology textbooks and is adequately discussed there. We will show here the relation between the orientation to educational achievement derived from emphasis on abilities and aptitudes and our own approach. In particular, it is necessary to call attention to some remarkable changes in the conceptualization of aptitudes and abilities that have occurred in recent years.

For the greater part of the twentieth century, thinking about educational achievement has been dominated by conceptions that in recent years have been subjected to vigorous attack. Foremost among these traditional views is the belief that individuals are endowed by their genetic inheritance with a native capacity for general intellectual achievement. At the extreme, this view postulates inborn intellectual skill which cannot be modified by learning experiences. Part of this belief is the conception that the intellectual ability of a child relative to other children of his age is virtually constant at different ages and that his IQ at a later age can be predicted from his IQ at an earlier age. Similar beliefs are held with respect to aptitudes regarded as components of intelligence, such as verbal fluency, perception of spatial relations, and reasoning ability, or special aptitudes such as artistic or musical talent.

These beliefs are no longer universally held, since it is recognized that no adequate proof exists for them. Moreover, studies of the intellectual development of a particular child over a period of years have demonstrated that considerable changes in intellectual performance relative to other children of the same age do occur. In addition, studies of animals placed in a severely restricted environment, as well as intensive studies of children, are leading to a profound reconceptualization of the nature of intelligence, of its components, and of other aptitudes.

At one time, if a child was failing in school it was customary to administer an intelligence test and, if he was shown to have a low score, to suggest that his poor performance was due simply to low native intelligence. While this practice still occurs with unwanted frequency, it is clear today that this explanation of poor academic performance is far from adequate. The customary distinction between tests of general intelligence and tests of educational achievement has become blurred. Intelligence tests were once thought to measure something close to native capacity or potential, and achievement tests to measure a person's present level of performance. Today it is no longer clear that each measures something different. It now seems probable that each measures only a particular kind of performance.

The point of view concerning the measurement of "capacity" taken by Anastasi, an outstanding contemporary authority on individual differences and psychological tests, is instructive:

> Another area of psychology in which confusions regarding heredity and environment are likely to arise is that of the interpretation of psychological tests. Persons unfamiliar with the way in which psychological tests are developed and used sometimes expect such tests to measure "native intelligence," "innate capacities," "hereditary predispositions of personality," and the like. By now it should be apparent that such expectations are sheer nonsense.

Between the biochemical properties of genes—which constitute the individual's heredity—and the complex functions subsumed under the headings of intelligence and personality there intervene a vast number of steps. At each step there occur intricate interactions involving environmental conditions—past and present—as well as any relevant indirect effects of specific genes. The end product reflects a multiplicity of influences, structural and functional, hereditary and environmental.

Every psychological test measures a sample of the individual's behavior. No test provides any special devices or "tricks" for penetrating beyond behavior or for eliminating the subject's past experiences. All conditions influencing behavior will inevitably be reflected in test scores. In so far as performance on a given test correlates with performance in other situations, the test can serve in diagnosing or predicting behavior. It is in this sense only that a psychological test can be said to measure "capacity" or "potentiality."

For example, we may be able to construct a test that will predict how well high school freshmen can learn French, before they have even begun the study of French. We would thus be testing the student's capacity for learning French rather than his present knowledge of the language. Such capacity, however, would be tested by determining how well the individual performs certain necessary prerequisite functions and how effectively he learns vocabulary and grammatical rules similar to those he will be taught in French classes. In other words, we would use the students' present performance in relevant tasks to predict how well each would do when taught a new language.

It is well to remember that whenever the terms "capacity" and "potentiality" are employed in reference to psychological tests, they are to be interpreted in the above sense of prediction. No psychological test measures genes! To ask that it do so simply reflects a misconception of the nature of heredity and of its role in behavior.[1]

The foregoing quotation makes clear that tests and other types of psychological measurement are simply devices for describing in quantitative terms a sample of the individual's behavior. Typically through the use of the correlation coefficient, such measurements may be used to predict educational achievement. Correlations are high and yield reasonably accurate predictions if persons who perform well on the test also perform well in school or on the job while those who perform poorly on the test do not. Correlations are low and of little predictive value when the test performance of each individual has little relation to his achievement in the school or job situation.

Even substantial correlations between educational achievement and a particular aptitude or personality trait, however, are subject

1. Anne Anastasi, *Differential Psychology*, 3rd ed. (New York: Macmillan, 1958), p. 82.

to several different interpretations. First and most common is the view that abilities, traits, habits, attitudes, or behavioral patterns, once formed, are somewhat autonomous and persistent from situation to situation. From this point of view an individual with certain personality traits is seen to succeed in school because these characteristics facilitate his academic performance. Thus, the direction of causation is from an intra-individual variable to academic performance.

A second view of associations between intra-individual characteristics and academic performance is opposite to the first: it holds that academic performance may to some degree shape the personality of the child in an appropriate direction. For example, a child who starts out well in school may respond by increasing his interest in reading and in other intellectual activities. This in turn will give him a somewhat higher score on a personality test for introversion. Even more obvious is the possibility that appropriate attitudes toward school subjects may be the result rather than the cause of good performance in school.

A third view is that both the cognitive abilities and the personality traits later found to be associated with academic performance develop concurrently with the various specific skills that result in good or poor performance. This view is supported by a recent study examining the relations between achievement motivation, intelligence-test scores, and performance in the grammar school selection tests taken at age eleven in Great Britain.[2] The study noted that a child's experiences of success and failure in academic work in primary school are related to his intellectual ability as well as to the amount of effort he expends. The intelligent child will experience more success; he thus is encouraged and rewarded, increasing the strength of the achievement motive, which in turn leads to further success. The empirical findings were consistent with this view: measures of need for achievement were found to correlate positively with intelligence. At the same time, each variable was shown to be independently associated with the child's performance on the grammar school selection tests. Thus, in this third view the direction of causation is from experiences of success or failure to performance on intelligence *and* on personality tests such as measures of the need for achievement.

---

2. W. P. Robinson, "The Achievement Motive, Academic Success and Intelligence Test Scores," *British Journal of Social and Clinical Psychology*, Vol. 4 (1965), pp. 98–103.

Probably all three viewpoints are correct in some instances; it is unlikely that just one interpretation would be consistent with all of the facts. These views are contrasted here to encourage open-mindedness in interpreting findings. It is only too easy to assume that intra-individual variables are *causes* of academic performance.

The contemporary view of the relation of abilities and personality traits to educational achievement, which we have sketched in the preceding pages, elevates social psychological processes to a position of major importance. Our view is that the educational performance of an individual at any stage is a function not only of his previous experiences with objects and ideas in his environment but also of his previous interactions with persons. Further, contemporary social processes prevailing during the assessment of his academic performance acquire significance. Traditional educational psychology has in the past given little attention to these matters.

Subsequent sections of this chapter deal with the relation between academic performance and the following topics: study habits and interests, achievement motivation, anxiety, introversion-extraversion, neuroticism and adjustment, and the self concept.

STUDY HABITS, ATTITUDES, AND INTERESTS

Most research on the effects on educational achievement of study habits and attitudes toward study has been conducted at the college level; few studies have been conducted at the high school level and none at the elementary level. The results obtained, however, are fairly consistent.[3] Students of comparable ability but having study habits ranging from poor to good differ significantly in academic performance. Positive attitudes toward intellectual pursuits and toward education in general are associated with better academic performance. Measures of interest in specific academic subjects, as well as more abstract interests such as preference for intellectual as opposed to social activities, have also been found to be associated with educational achievement, when ability is controlled or equated. However, conceptualization here is somewhat vague, and it is difficult to interpret some attitude or interest measures. For example, an individual may express a preference for certain academic subjects,

---

3. D. E. Lavin, *The Prediction of Academic Performance* (New York: Russell Sage Foundation, 1965).

not because of their intrinsic interest, but because they lead to high-status occupations; in that instance his preferences represent social ambitions rather than an intellectual attitude. Or a person may be attracted toward social activities because he is bored by academic pursuits, not because he is especially gregarious. Thus, even when attitude and interest measures are clearly shown to relate to academic achievement, the meaning of such findings is not easy to interpret.

ACHIEVEMENT MOTIVATION

The concept of *achievement motivation* has received much attention from psychologists in recent years. It refers to the need of an individual to perform according to a high standard of excellence. It follows from this definition that a high association should be expected between the level of achievement motivation and academic performance. Because achievement motivation is correlated with intelligence, the relation between it and academic performance should be studied with the level of intelligence controlled.[4]

Earlier research programs emphasized the measurement of achievement motivation by "projective" methods in which a student was shown a series of pictures and asked to compose a story in response to each of them. The greater the number of achievement themes in the stories, the higher was the achievement motivation attributed to the child. More recently, however, questionnaires or self-inventory measures of achievement have been used more frequently. In addition, behavioral measures of achievement have received more emphasis. Here the stress is on standards of excellence,

---

4. Early studies found little relation between intelligence and achievement motivation: D. C. McClelland, J. W. Atkinson, R. A. Clark, and E. L. Lowell, *The Achievement Motive* (New York: Appleton-Century-Crofts, 1953); D. C. McClelland, "Methods of Measuring Human Motivation," in J. W. Atkinson, ed., *Motives in Fantasy, Action, and Society* (Princeton: Van Nostrand, 1958). But Robinson points out that, in these early investigations, the range of intelligence was severely restricted by the use of American male college students as subjects, markedly attenuating any possible correlation coefficients that might prevail in a sample more representative of the IQ range of the population (see fn. 2). Kagan and Moss have reported a positive association between the need achievement scores of eight-year-old children and the increase in IQ exhibited by these children from age six to age ten (J. Kagan and H. A. Moss, "The Stability and Validity of Achievement Fantasy," *Journal of Abnormal and Social Psychology*, Vol. 58 [1959], pp. 357–64). Robinson also reports a correlation of .40 between need achievement and IQ for a large sample of eleven-year-old British children.

competent performance, and concern over the approval of such performances.[5]

As in many other investigations of academic performance, most research has been carried out at the college level. Of those studies examining the relation between achievement motivation as measured by projective devices and academic performance, only about half yield a positive association. Achievement motivation assessed by questionnaires such as the Edwards Personal Preference Schedule showed more consistent correlations with educational achievement,[6] but even these studies produced some conflicting and unstable results. In 1962, researchers found low but positive correlations between need achievement, as measured by the Edwards Schedule, and academic performance, with intelligence controlled.[7] However, a follow-up study in 1966 failed to confirm these results in most respects.[8]

Another study, using eight different measures of achievement motivation, suggests some possible reasons for these diverse findings.[9] This investigation employed a statistical technique called factor analysis, a technique that identifies the main dimensions or components that underlie test items. Achievement motivation as customarily measured was found to consist of several different dimensions or components, including academic motivation and efficiency, self-satisfaction, wish-fulfillment motivation, nonacademic achievement orientation, and external pressures to achieve. Thus, many measures of achievement motivation include nonacademic components which should not be expected to correlate with academic performance. In addition, projective devices apparently measure achievement fantasies that often have little relation to actual behavior. Academic motivation and efficiency were found in this study

5. V. J. Crandall, "Achievement," in H. W. Stevenson, ed., *Child Psychology: The Sixty-second Yearbook of the National Society for the Study of Education, Part I* (Chicago: University of Chicago Press, 1963), pp. 416–59.

6. Allen Edwards, *Edwards Personal Preference Schedule* (New York: Psychological Corporation, 1954).

7. L. D. Goodstein and A. B. Heilbrun, Jr., "Prediction of College Achievement from the Edwards Personal Preference Schedule at Three Levels of Intellectual Ability," *Journal of Applied Psychology*, Vol. 46 (1962), pp. 317–20.

8. M. D. Hakel, "Prediction of College Achievement from the Edwards Personal Preference Schedule Using Intellectual Ability as a Moderator," *Journal of Applied Psychology*, Vol. 50 (1966), pp. 336–40.

9. J. V. Mitchell, Jr., "An Analysis of the Factorial Dimensions of the Achievement Motivation Construct, *Journal of Educational Psychology*, Vol. 52 (1961), pp. 179–87.

to be best measured by objective questionnaires. Moreover, academic and extracurricular achievements have only negligible correlations with each other; [10] thus, some individuals with high achievement motivation may find satisfaction in extracurricular activities and perform poorly on academic tests.

Another plausible explanation of the low correlations between achievement motivation and academic performance is that other variables may operate concurrently with achievement motivation to suppress or to facilitate its operation. For example, some persons with high achievement motivation may also fear failure to an extent that impedes their performance. The presence of this fear in an appreciable number of students would attenuate correlations between achievement motivation and academic performance.

ANXIETY

Some investigators have asked whether general anxiety, such as is measured by the Taylor Manifest Anxiety Scale,[11] a self-inventory, is related to academic performance. Sample questions from this inventory are given below, together with the responses scored as "anxious":

I work under a great deal of strain. (True)
At times I lose sleep over worry. (True)
When embarrassed I often break out in a sweat which is very annoying. (True)

This notion of general anxiety assumes a relatively constant level of tension within the individual; this level is measured indirectly by questions about symptoms indicative of such tension.

Other research explores the relation between educational achievement and anxiety specific to test-taking situations. Here, the questionnaire elicits agreement or disagreement with statements about tension and its effects in test-taking situations. For example:

During exams or tests, I block on questions to which I know the answers, even though I might remember them as soon as the exam is over. (Agree)
I find that my mind goes blank at the beginning of an exam, and it takes me a few minutes before I can function. (Agree)

10. J. L. Holland and J. M. Richards, Jr., "Academic and Nonacademic Accomplishment: Correlated or Uncorrelated?" *Journal of Educational Psychology*, Vol. 56 (1965), pp. 165–74.
11. J. A. Taylor, "A Personality Scale of Manifest Anxiety," *Journal of Abnormal Social Psychology*, Vol. 48 (1953), pp. 285–90.

This approach assumes that an individual's level of anxiety varies in different situations and that measures of anxiety specifically associated with test-taking situations will have a more marked association with academic performance than will measures of general anxiety.

On the college level, most studies report zero or low negative correlations between general anxiety and academic performance. In a few studies, however, where several different measures of ability and personality were correlated with educational achievement, the inclusion of a measure of general anxiety raised the overall correlation [12] between these measures and academic achievement: the lower the anxiety, the better the performance. Below the college level, research is insufficient to draw any firm conclusions concerning general anxiety levels.

In contrast to general anxiety, anxiety specific to test-taking situations is more consistently related to test performance on all educational levels: again, the higher the anxiety, the lower the performance, when ability level is controlled. The association is not great; correlations are quite low but are nearly always in the predicted direction. Longitudinal studies of test-taking anxiety in the early grades yield some further information.[13] Little relation between anxiety and educational achievement exists in the first grade. Correlations become increasingly negative with each successive grade, with the highest negative correlation obtained for the highest grade studied, the fifth grade. The more anxious a pupil is, the less well he performs. Although measures of anxiety are moderately stable over two-year intervals, correlation between first-grade and fifth-grade anxiety is negligible. Those children who are anxious in the first grade are not necessarily anxious in the fifth grade. Increases in anxiety over the years are associated with poorer academic performance; reductions in anxiety have the opposite effect.

---

12. The "overall correlation" is more technically described as a multiple correlation coefficient.
13. S. B. Sarason, K. T. Hill, and P. Zimbardo, "A Longitudinal Study of the Relation of Test Anxiety to Performance on Intelligence and Achievement Tests," *Monographs of the Society for Research in Child Development*, Vol. 29 (Whole No. 98), No. 7 (1964), pp. 1–51; K. T. Hill and S. B. Sarason, "The Relation of Test Anxiety and Defensiveness to Test and School Performance over the Elementary-School Years: A Further Longitudinal Study," *Monographs of the Society for Research in Child Development*, Vol. 31 (Whole No. 104), No. 2 (1966), pp. 1–76.

Anxiety is also more associated with achievement in reading than in arithmetic. Over this period of time, boys report anxiety to a decreasing extent, but this decrease is associated with an increasing reluctance to *report* such experiences and perhaps a refusal to admit them to oneself. Girls report the opposite; for them, anxiety increases with progression through the grades. Probably this is a function of the difference in age-sex roles: *admitting* that one is anxious is more appropriate for girls.

The many college-level studies of general and test-taking anxiety in relation to academic performance suggest that the relation between these variables is not a simple linear one, that instead it is a complex "curvilinear" function, and that it is perhaps further complicated by the effects of other variables. One form of curvilinearity is illustrated by the case where a virtual absence of anxiety is associated with a lack of motivation to perform well, while a moderate amount of anxiety is a stimulant to good performance and a high level of anxiety interferes with performance. Evidence for precisely this relation between anxiety and performance has been presented in a study comparing performance on a moderately complex task with a measure of general anxiety.[14] Yet, many investigators studying anxiety and achievement use statistical procedures which assume that the relation between these measures is *not* curvilinear. These procedures misleadingly make it appear that no relation exists.

A number of studies[15] demonstrate that individuals high in general anxiety memorize easy paired-associates (for example, table-chair; black-white) more readily than do individuals low in anxiety but that the reverse is true for more difficult memorizing tasks. These findings at first suggested that general anxiety acted as a motivating stimulus which facilitated learning of *easy* tasks but interfered with learning of *difficult* tasks. More recent evidence sug-

---

14. R. Lynn and I. E. Gordon, "The Relation of Neuroticism and Extraversion to Intelligence and Educational Attainment," *British Journal of Educational Psychology*, Vol. 31 (1961), pp. 194–203.

15. J. A. Taylor and J. P. Chapman, "Paired-Associate Learning as Related to Anxiety," *American Journal of Psychology*, Vol. 68 (1955), p. 671; K. W. Spence, J. A. Taylor, and R. Ketchel, "Anxiety (Drive) Level and Degree of Competition in Paired-Associates Learning," *Journal of Experimental Psychology*, Vol. 52 (1956), pp. 306–10; K. W. Spence, I. E. Farber, and H. H. McFann, "The Relation of Anxiety (Drive) Level to Performance in Competitional and Non-competitional Paired-Associates Learning," *Journal of Experimental Psychology*, Vol. 52 (1956), pp. 296–305.

gests that the different reactions of "high- and low-anxious" individuals to easy and difficult tasks is a consequence of differing reactions to experiences of success and failure.[16] High-anxious persons
do well on easy tasks because they respond well to their experiences
of success on such tasks, but they do poorly on difficult tasks because
their early experiences of failure interfere with subsequent performance. On the other hand, low-anxious persons respond to failure by
increasing their efforts and to success by slacking off. Other investigations are consistent with these interpretations of performances of high- and low-anxious individuals on easy and difficult
tasks.[17]

Another study covering a period of years indicates that the relation between general anxiety and performance in college is complicated by aptitude, by study habits, and by changing academic
standards.[18] Anxiety was found to facilitate the academic performance of upperclassmen of especially *high* ability but not the performance of those with *low* or *average* ability. Those of high ability
experience success, which stimulates them to further achievement;
the remaining students experience difficulties and failures, which
further impair their performance under tension. Data collected
several years later at the same school yielded somewhat different results: high anxiety impaired performance. This was explained by

---

16. Bernard Weiner, "Role of Success and Failure in the Learning of Easy and
   Complex Tasks," *Journal of Personality and Social Psychology,* Vol. 3, No.
   3 (1966), pp. 339–44.
17. Several studies support the idea that, following success, highly anxious individuals improve their performance, while failure impairs their future
   performance: I. L. Child and J. W. M. Whiting, "Effects of Goal Attainment: Relaxation Versus Renewed Striving," *Journal of Abnormal and Social Psychology,* Vol. 45 (1950), pp. 667–81; L. T. Katchmar, S. Ross, and
   T. G. Andrews, "Effects of Stress and Anxiety on Performance of a Complex Verbal-Coding Task," *Journal of Experimental Psychology,* Vol. 55
   (1958), pp. 559–63; J. D. Lucas, "The Interactive Effects of Anxiety, Failure,
   and Interserial Duplication," *American Journal of Psychology,* Vol. 55 (1952),
   pp. 59–66; G. Mandler and S. B. Sarason, "A Study of Anxiety and Learning," *Journal of Abnormal and Social Psychology,* Vol. 47 (1952), pp. 166–
   73; S. B. Sarason, "The Effects of Anxiety and Two Kinds of Failure on
   Serial Learning," *Journal of Personality,* Vol. 25 (1957), pp. 383–92; Bernard
   Weiner, "The Effects of Unsatisfied Achievement Motivation on Persistence
   and Subsequent Performance," *Journal of Personality,* Vol. 33 (1965), pp.
   428–42.
18. C. D. Spielberger and H. Weitz, "Improving the Academic Performance
   of Anxious College Freshmen," *Psychological Monograph,* Vol. 78 (Whole
   No. 590), No. 13 (1964).

an increase in academic standards and in competition, caused by more stringent admission procedures. Even for the high-ability freshmen, performance at an acceptable level was no longer easy, and anxiety was not facilitative.

To sum up, we can say that a basic principle seems to underlie most of the research on anxiety and academic performance: where a student anticipates success, anxiety facilitates performance; where he expects to fail, anxiety impedes performance. Thus, the absence of anxiety better enables an average student to cope with difficult assignments, but it is apt to lead to reduced effort when assignments are easy. In like manner, the ability of the student relates to anxiety and performance. The able student may benefit from anxiety because assignments are not too difficult for him and he anticipates success; but the performance of the student of low ability is impeded by anxiety because he anticipates failure.

OTHER PERSONALITY TRAITS

Numerous studies [19] in England and the United States support the generalization that introversion is associated with academic performance, although there are some exceptions.[20] Students in high school and college who are more introverted generally do better at academic tasks. The interpretation of these findings is less certain than that concerning anxiety. Suggested explanations include the following: (1) Introverts form conditioned responses more rapidly than extraverts, suggesting that they learn more quickly. (2) Intro-

---

19. W. D. Furneaux, "Report to Imperial College of Science and Technology," 1956, cited in Robinson, *op. cit.;* D. E. Broadbent, *Perception and Communication* (London: Pergamon Press, 1958); A. W. Bendig, "Extraversion, Neuroticism, and Student Achievement in Introductory Psychology," *Journal of Educational Research,* Vol. 53 (1960), pp. 263–67; Lynn and Gordon, *op. cit.;* R. D. Savage, "Personality Factors and Academic Performance," *British Journal of Educational Psychology,* Vol. 32 (1962), pp. 251–53; H. J. Butcher, M. Ainsworth, and J. E. Nesbitt, "Personality Factors and School Achievement: A Comparison of British and American Children," *British Journal of Educational Psychology,* Vol. 33 (1963), pp. 276–85; K. W. Haun, "A Note on the Prediction of Academic Performance from Personality-Test Scores," *Psychological Reports,* Vol. 16 (1965), p. 294; Paul Kline, "Extraversion, Neuroticism and Academic Performance Among Ghanaian University Students," *British Journal of Educational Psychology,* Vol. 36 (1966), pp. 92–94.
20. R. D. Savage, "Personality Factors and Academic Attainment in Junior School Children," *British Journal of Educational Psychology,* Vol. 36 (1966), pp. 91–92.

verts are more capable of sustained concentration or attention to work. (3) Introverts devote more time to study than extraverts. (4) Introverts tend to tackle complex tasks slowly and accurately, while extraverts are quicker and less accurate.[21] Also worth considering is the possibility that success in academic pursuits may encourage behavior consistent with items in a test of introversion-extraversion—reading and studying are solitary activities.

The relation between academic performance and such general traits as neuroticism and adjustment has also been studied. Neuroticism as measured by some self-inventories is highly correlated with measures of general anxiety; thus, findings are apt to be inconsistent for the reasons we discussed under the topic of anxiety. There are many complications in relating academic performance to neuroticism and anxiety.[22] Measures of adjustment are even more heterogeneous: they may include test items pertaining to anxiety, self-esteem, introversion-extraversion, and other personality traits. It would be unreasonable to expect consistent results from studies employing these different measures.

SELF AND ACADEMIC ACHIEVEMENT

It is a uniquely human characteristic that a person becomes an object to himself. Because he possesses language and high intelligence, man has a unique capacity for thinking about his body, his behavior, and his appearance to other persons. Each of us has a set of judgments, thoughts, and feelings about ourselves. These elements are commonly referred to as the *self* or *self concept*. These notions of self are generated primarily through interaction and communication with other persons—*the self is a social product*. Two features are essential to the formation of a self concept: first, the individual must perceive how he is judged by other persons around him. These judgments may be explicit, as when a mother tells her son that he is "a bad boy," or they may be quite indirect, as when an individual interprets a slight gesture by another person as disapproval of some act or characteristic of his. The concept of "the looking-glass self" [23]

21. Lynn and Gordon, *op. cit.*

22. J. B. Biggs, "The Relation of Neuroticism and Extraversion to Intelligence and Educational Attainment," *British Journal of Educational Psychology*, Vol. 32 (1962), pp. 188–95.

23. C. H. Cooley, *Human Nature and the Social Order* (New York: Scribner's, 1902).

epitomizes this process very nicely—an individual derives a reflected view of himself from the actions of others toward him. A second and important feature of the formation of the self concept is that the individual *compares* this reflection of self against a standard, a set of expectations that he and others hold as to how he *should* behave and what characteristics he *should* have. If the judgment he imputes to others exceeds the standard, he is likely to feel proud; if it falls below this standard, he may be ashamed.

This concept of self plays an important role in many personality theories. Some behavioral scientists believe that, once the self concept is firmly established, the individual strives to behave in a manner that is consistent with it. While there is probably some validity to this view, there are many interaction processes involving the social environment of the individual that help to maintain *both* self and behavior.[24] Thus, self should not always be thought of as an antecedent cause of behavior that is consistent with it; a more appropriate interpretation may be that self and behavior are both effects of some larger social process. For example, a person may think of himself as a capable student and also do well in school. Either his self concept or his performance *could* be the antecedent cause, but another possibility is that both his self concept and his performance develop together as a result of favorable learning conditions and experiences.

Over two decades ago, Lecky suggested that a student's self concept determines how well he performs in school.[25] His particular focus was the student's ideas of his abilities and capacities. Experiences in primary school, he believed, established in the student certain beliefs about his own capacities. This was particularly likely to occur among students whose failure or success was outstanding. For example, many students at the college level are poor spellers, even though their accomplishments in other respects are at a high level. In Lecky's analysis it seemed unlikely that poor spelling in such students reflected capacity; more probable was a fixed conviction on the part of the student that he simply could not spell—a conviction that left him helpless and without the motivation to correct the deficiency. In writing a theme, such individuals misspelled

24. P. F. Secord and C. W. Backman, "Personality Theory and the Problem of Stability and Change in Individual Behavior," *Psychological Review*, Vol. 68 (1961), pp. 21–32.
25. Prescott Lecky, *Self-consistency: A Theory of Personality* (New York: Island Press, 1945).

approximately the same number of words on each page, even though they sometimes spelled a word right and sometimes wrong. Such performance might be accounted for by a student's need for consistency between his conception of self and his performance—with a failure to be consistent leading to confusion and dismay. Lecky's own therapeutic approach to this problem was, in a series of intensive sessions, to point up the inconsistency between thinking of oneself as a poor speller but as good at history, mathematics, or whatever subjects were appropriate. Some students responded remarkably well to this therapy; some even went on to win spelling championships in highly competitive contests.

In recent years, research on the relation between the self concept and academic performance has attempted to test such ideas. At present the answers are not conclusive, although considerable progress has been made.

One general measure of self is *self-esteem.* Here the focus is upon the degree to which an individual evaluates himself favorably in terms of what he and other persons important to him consider socially desirable. In fourth- and sixth-grade boys self-esteem and academic achievement have been shown to be positively correlated to a significant degree.[26] Correlations for girls, however, are much lower and generally are not statistically significant. Academic achievement is often less important for girls and plays a lesser role in their self-esteem than it does for boys.

Another possible interpretation of this study, however, is that both self-esteem and performance in school are effects of intelligence. Highly intelligent pupils might do well *because* they are intelligent, and they might have high self-esteem *because* they are intelligent; the reverse might be true for pupils of low intelligence. If this accounted for all of the observed relation between self-esteem and academic performance, it would mean that self-esteem is not the *cause* of good academic performance. We have, however, applied to the data above the statistical technique of partial correlation, to remove the effect of intelligence from the correlation between self-esteem and academic performance.[27] The correlation for fourth-

---

26. J. C. Bledsoe, "Self Concepts of Children and Their Intelligence, Achievement, Interests, and Anxiety," *Journal of Individual Psychology,* Vol. 20 (May 1964), pp. 55–58.

27. Since it was not provided in the study, it was necessary to estimate the correlation between intelligence and achievement. This was estimated at .40 for the purpose of computing partial correlation.

grade boys remained approximately the same; for sixth-graders, only a slight drop occurred. We may conclude that the correlation between self-esteem and academic performance is genuine. One other caution should be kept in mind: it is possible that good performance in school leads to self-esteem, rather than the other way around. More extensive studies reported below will have some relevance to this question.

A series of studies of the self concept and educational achievement are now under way, following the progress of a particular group of students over a period of years and noting changes in self concept and performance. By means of such data, it should be possible to determine whether the self can be treated as antecedent to academic performance or merely as a correlate or an effect of the level of performance. Unlike research which deals with *general* self-esteem, these studies concentrate on the student's *academic self concept,* which consists of his responses to multiple-choice items concerning his beliefs about his ability to succeed in various academic subjects. Appreciable correlations have been found between this self concept and academic performance in mathematics, science, and social studies for seventh-grade boys but only in social studies for girls.[28] This is consistent with findings that academic performance has more self-relevance for boys than for girls. Moreover, these correlations remain appreciable even when actual ability is controlled.

A follow-up study amasses further evidence for an association between the self concept and academic performance.[29] An association between the self concept and academic achievement has been demonstrated in the same students from the seventh through the tenth grades, and changes in self concept over this three-year period have been related to changes in academic performance. Also involved here is the concept of *reflected self* [30]—an individual's estimate of how persons important to him would describe him. The theory that the self is social and that it grows out of interactions between

28. W. B. Brookover, S. Thomas, and A. Paterson, "Self Concept of Ability and School Achievement," *Sociology of Education,* Vol. 37 (1964), pp. 271–79.

29. W. B. Brookover, J. M. LePere, E. L. Erickson, and S. Thomas, "Definitions of Others, Self Concept, and Academic Achievement: A Longitudinal Study," paper presented at American Sociological Association, Chicago, August 1965.

30. C. W. Backman and P. F. Secord, "Liking, Selective Interaction, and Misperception in Congruent Interpersonal Relations," *Sociometry,* Vol. 25 (1962), pp. 321–35.

an individual and persons around him suggests that a student's parents, friends, and teachers see him in the way he sees himself. This study provides some evidence that, from the seventh to the tenth grades, the selves reflected by parents, teachers, and friends become increasingly similar to the student's views of himself.

The effect of the reflected self on performance was nicely demonstrated by the work of Rosenthal and Jacobson.[31] In 18 classrooms, ranging from the first to the sixth grades, they administered a nonverbal IQ test represented by them as being able to predict academic blooming. Following this, they reported to the teachers the names of approximately 20 percent of the children, whom they predicted would make unusual intellectual gains during the coming year. The children reported were actually chosen at random, without regard to their test performance. Yet, eight months later, their actual performance on the same nonverbal IQ test revealed greater gains than for the children not named. This effect was especially pronounced in the lower grades. Presumably this effect would have been even greater on an academic-achievement test. Thus, it is clear that somehow the teacher's expectations of intellectual progress by the designated children led them to perform better on a test relatively unrelated to school subjects. A reasonable assumption is that teacher expectations shaped the children's self concept in a way that produced a performance consistent with this self concept. Unfortunately, the investigators did not use any measure of self, which would have permitted a more direct test of this assumption.

It is clear that the self concept and academic performance are correlated; yet, at the present writing the most important question has not been fully answered. No researcher has proved that the concept of self held by an individual appreciably sets the level of his future performance. It could well be that the self concept is more a reflection of how the individual has performed in the past. However, when partial correlation was used to remove the effects of memory for past performance from current performance and current self concept, appreciable correlations remained.[32] This suggests that the self concept does have at least some effect upon future performance.

31. R. Rosenthal and L. Jacobson, "Teachers' Expectancies: Determinants of Pupils' IQ Gains," *Psychological Reports*, Vol. 19 (1966), pp. 115–18.
32. Brookover *et al., op. cit.*

Implications for the Classroom

The most important point made in this chapter is the increased emphasis on experience and on social factors as determinants of ability and performance. In part because of the nature of our language, and in part because it is easier, we tend to see the behavior of a person as a function of qualities that inhere in him. A man commits a crime because he has a "criminal mind," or a soldier performs a heroic deed because he is "brave." In the same way, we see a student as performing well because he is intelligent or doing poorly because he is stupid or because he does not try. Too often we ignore the situation or circumstances that lead a person to behave as he does, and we give even less attention to the effect of his previous experience on his performance.

As children grow older, their various abilities level off within some narrowly defined range. Most older children and adults do not show much change in test performance. It was this phenomenon that led psychologists to believe that ability levels are rooted in neuro-physiological properties of the organism. But there are cogent arguments for the view that this stabilization of abilities is largely a function of motivational and personality factors, rather than of any inherent qualities of the individual. The proverb "nothing succeeds like success" expresses one form of argument. The child who succeeds in particular kinds of performances is apt to be encouraged by others and to experience self-satisfaction in such performances. This leads him to maintain and to develop further his skills in those areas in which he is successful. On the other hand, those other activities in which he is conspicuously inept may well be avoided or abandoned altogether. For example, a person who, throughout his childhood, has been a notoriously poor speller is not likely to adopt a determined campaign to improve his spelling—he has long since resigned himself to his handicap. But there are a minority of individuals whose life situation changes sufficiently so that they adopt drastically new attitudes toward themselves and their performances. Such individuals often undergo a remarkable development in mental abilities and skills, a development that is largely a function of their new aspirations. The case histories of such persons provide our best evidence for the role of social and motivational factors in performances requiring ability and skill.

This increased emphasis on experience and motivation has a profound implication for education. Teachers should resist the temptation to write off certain children as hopeless and others as capable of only mediocre performance. These actions are apt to amount to a "self-fulfilling prophecy"—the teacher's expectations create mediocre performance. Such children need more attention, not less. Ways have to be found to provide them with experiences that they have been deprived of and to generate their interest in the subject matter to be learned. This is easier said than done, of course. Most teachers have too many pupils to be able to give sufficient attention to those who need it most. Quite possibly, further developments in computerization and other forms of mechanized education will provide remedial opportunities for such pupils and also give the teacher more time to spend with individual pupils.

Also clear from our discussion is the necessity for maintaining anxiety at an optimum level for each individual. When faced with difficult tasks, pupils of low or moderate ability can experience anxiety that seriously hampers their performance. For such pupils, teachers should learn to avoid arousing anxiety concerning difficult tasks. Especially able pupils, on the other hand, benefit if they are given challenging tasks. The pacing of learning is important here, not only to maintain anxiety at a low level but also from the standpoint of efficient learning.

We need more educational research on the structure of the curriculum—we have to know the kinds and amounts of experiences that children need in order to develop abilities and skills. Our present curricula in the elementary grades may be grossly inefficient, for all we can tell. Certain classroom experiences may have negative instead of positive effects upon future performance, others may have no effect, and some may be absolutely essential for future development. The "new math" curriculum is an attempt to restructure curricula in an appropriate direction, but it is based on theoretical notions that have not been thoroughly tested by studying children. With appropriate and intensive research, we may some day be able to pace the child's educational training so that he moves from one step to another with ease, and so that children in general perform at a much higher level than does the average child today.

In summary, virtually all the research we have reviewed leads to the conclusion that the most important factor in educational achievement is that the child must repeatedly experience success in his school endeavors. This builds appropriate abilities, study habits, attitudes, and values and minimizes those factors that interfere with performance.

Chapter Three

The School Setting

Chapters One and Two have dealt with social class, family, ability, and personality as they relate to student performance. Here we examine the school setting itself. We will discuss as major topics the effects on the individual of the attitudes and aspirations of the student body, the curriculum, living groups, friends, and faculty members.

LEARNING ENVIRONMENTS
OF HIGH SCHOOLS AND COLLEGES

The school may be viewed as a miniature society, having its own culture or climate, which in turn is made up of a variety of identifiable subcultures that affect the behavior and performance of the student in various ways. Most studies of this aspect of the school have, unfortunately, dealt only with the college level. A few have been made in high schools, but none in elementary schools. In high schools and colleges these studies revealed marked differences in the pressures exerted by faculty and students for academic performance, in the intellectual, political, and social orientation of the students, and in the students' educational aspirations. Whether similar differences exist at the elementary level will not be known until specific studies are made of elementary schools. These differences have been examined in relation to three classes of variables: (1) the informal structure and culture of the student body; (2) characteristics of the school—its size, its type of program, its faculty; and (3) background and personal characteristics of the students.

On the college level, marked differences among the environments of colleges and universities have been demonstrated.[1] Stern and his associates have conceived of the institutional environment in terms of environmental press. This concept refers to the environment experienced by the person—the actions and values he is exposed to. Pressures arise from several sources: (1) through his observation of faculty members or older students who serve as models and whom he wishes to imitate, (2) from more direct attempts by other persons to influence his attitudes and behavior, and (3) through his view of the prevailing attitudes and values of the faculty and student body. A measure of press is obtained from the College Characteristics Inventory (CCI), a 300-item objective questionnaire in which the student, in effect, describes the school environment as he sees it.[2] The interschool differences listed below are typical of those obtained from this questionnaire.

A New England, Private, Liberal Arts College for Girls

Intellectuality. The marked intellectual needs and aspirations of these girls are very strongly supported by the press at this school. They all agree that many of the professors are actively engaged in research, and that many students are actively pursuing careers in science. There are also especially strong facilities in the humanities, however, and the students express their interests in art, music, and the theater in many different ways. Long, serious intellectual discussions are common here. There is also much concern with values, and the expression of strong personal convictions is not uncommon. No one needs to be afraid of expressing extreme or unpopular viewpoints at this school. It has an excellent reputation for academic freedom.

Most of the professors are dedicated scholars and thorough teachers. They put a lot of energy into their teaching. Most courses are a

---

1. C. R. Pace and G. G. Stern, "An Approach to the Measurement of Psychological Characteristics of College Environments," *Journal of Educational Psychology*, Vol. 49 (1958), pp. 269–77; D. L. Thistlethwaite, "College Press and Student Achievement," *Journal of Educational Psychology*, Vol. 50 (1959), pp. 183–91; A. W. Astin and J. L. Holland, "The Environmental Assessment Technique. A Way to Measure College Environments," *Journal of Educational Psychology*, Vol. 52 (1961), pp. 308–16; A. W. Astin, " 'Productivity' of Undergraduate Institutions," *Science*, Vol. 136 (1962), pp. 129–35; "An Empirical Characterization of Higher Educational Institutions," *Journal of Educational Psychology*, Vol. 53 (1962), pp. 224–35; Martin Trow, "Student Cultures and Administrative Action," in R. L. Sutherland, W. H. Holtzman, E. A. Koile, and B. K. Smith, eds., *Personality Factors on the College Campus* (Austin: University of Texas Press, 1962), pp. 203–26; J. A. Davis, "Intellectual Climates in 135 American Colleges and Universities: A Study in 'Social Psychophysics,' " *Sociology of Education*, Vol. 37 (1963), pp. 110–28.
2. Pace and Stern, *op. cit.*

real intellectual challenge, requiring intensive study and preparation out of class. Tutorial and honors programs are available for qualified students. Professors and students both set high standards and work hard to achieve them, and the competition for grades is intense. If a student fails a course, however, he can usually substitute another one for it.

In class discussions, papers, and exams, the main emphasis is on breadth of understanding, perspective, and critical judgment, and a well-reasoned report can rate an "A" grade here even though its viewpoint is opposed to the professor's. The faculty members are liberal in interpreting regulations; they respect the students' motives, and treat violations with understanding and tolerance. Few students have special good luck charms or practices.

Dependency Needs. The intense rationality of this environment is further reflected in the thorough planning and organization that characterize most courses. However, students do not have assigned seats, and class attendance is neither taken nor required. An easy informality prevails between students and staff: faculty members, administrators, and counselors are always available and personally interested in the students, call them by their first names, and do not expect to be addressed as "professor" or "doctor." The students are treated with dignity and respect: they don't have to answer a lot of embarrassing questions when in need of help, tests are infrequent, grades are not posted publicly or reported to parents, written permission to leave campus overnight is not required, and freshmen don't have to take orders from upperclassmen. Students are encouraged to be independent and individualistic, and there is a high degree of respect for nonconformity and intellectual freedom: students are encouraged in many ways to criticize administrative policies and teaching practices. Religious worship does not stress service and obedience, and chapel services are not well attended. Although students will do things for which they know they may be criticized, they commonly share their problems and are rarely noisy or inattentive at concerts or lectures.

Impulse Expression. Courses stress the speculative or abstract, rather than the practical, and students are encouraged in their daydreams about varied or unusual careers. There is little interest or activity involving charities, community service, or concern with the underprivileged.

There are no social formalities or privileges here: there is no emphasis on tradition, proper social forms or manners, grooming, or various kinds of gracious living. On nice days many classes meet on the lawn. The students are serious and purposeful, spend much time at their studies, and local social activities are rare. Students frequently go away for football games or skiing weekends. There are no sororities.

Student rooms are likely to be decorated with art forms, and there is much interest here in all forms of esthetic experience on the part of students and staff. The students are impulsive and excitable, and student parties are colorful. Vivid and novel expressions in papers and reports are encouraged. Rough games and contact sports are an important part of intramural athletics. Channels for expressing student complaints are readily accessible, and when students do not like an administrative decision they really work to get it changed.[3]

A Southern, Coeducational, State University

At this school there are relatively few items concerned with *intellectuality* or *dependency needs*. The students agree that the libraries are good and the faculty is impartial. There is some emphasis on neatness, and the staff is addressed deferentially, but the students don't feel that the courses are well organized and they are rather critical of the faculty. The most important relationships appear to be between the students themselves, who borrow and share things, bring their problems to one another, help one another with their lessons, and prepare for examinations together.

This student togetherness is even more clearly delineated in the areas related to *impulse expression:*

Although the students all agree that the emphasis is on job security, personal adjustment, family happiness, and good citizenship, and that there are many really practical courses to this end in typing, report writing, human relations, etc., the major portion of the high-consensus items deal with another aspect of the press. They all agree that there is much to do at this school besides going to classes and studying. Every year there are carnivals, parades, and other festive events on campus. There are many fraternities and sororities, and receptions, teas, and formal dances occur frequently. Students give much thought to dressing appropriately and interestingly for different occasions—classes, social events, sports, and other affairs. There is a lot of excitement and restlessness just before holidays, and students frequently go away for football games, skiing weekends, and similar activities. Most students really enjoy dancing.

There are frequent informal social gatherings and it's easy to get a group together for card games, singing, or going to the movies. Dormitory raids, water fights, and other student pranks are not uncommon. Students spend a lot of time together at the snack bars, taverns, and in one another's rooms. There is lots of informal dating during the week—at the library, snack bar, or movies—and there are several popular spots where a crowd of boys and girls can always be found. These student gathering places are typically active and noisy.[4]

Although all campuses share certain characteristics, five patterns or clusters of characteristics in which colleges are apt to differ have been observed:

---

3. G. G. Stern, "Environments for Learning," in Nevitt Sanford, ed., *The American College* (New York: Wiley, 1962), pp. 690–730.

4. Stern, *op. cit.*, pp. 724–25.

The first two are both strongly intellectual, with one more strongly oriented toward humanism, sentience, and reflectiveness, and the other more strongly oriented toward scientism, uncertainty, and competition. The third cluster emphasizes the practical and applied rather than the abstract or theoretical, and is heavily concerned with establishing status in relation to peers and accepting status in relation to authority. The fourth cluster exhibits a strong press toward group welfare, human relations, and social responsibility. And the fifth cluster suggests a rebellion against the well-managed, group-welfare-oriented community.[5]

Schools differ in the relative prominence of these various clusters. A comparison of Antioch College, a private, Midwestern, coeducational, liberal-arts institution, with Vassar College, a private, Eastern, girls' liberal-arts school, produced the following observations:

> In both colleges the intellectual-humanistic-scientific clusters emerge as the strongest emphasis in the environment, with the practical, status-oriented cluster being correspondingly low. At Vassar the rebellion emphasis is about average. At Antioch the social welfare emphasis is about average. Rebellion is somewhat higher at Antioch and social welfare is somewhat lower at Vassar. Comparing the two schools, one finds Antioch having the stronger scientific press, and also being higher in rebellion and in social welfare.[6]

In contrast, Syracuse University, a larger, private, Eastern institution, is high on the practical, status-oriented dimensions and low on humanism and scientism. Compared to other institutions, it is average in its emphasis on social welfare but high on the rebellion cluster.

Trow has analyzed the climates of campus environments, which appear to vary in prominence from college to college, in terms of four subcultures: the collegiate culture, the vocational culture, the academic culture, and the nonconformist culture.[7] The *collegiate* culture he describes as a "world of football, fraternities and sororities, dates, cars and drinking, and campus fun." Participants in this subculture identify with their university as a social object, but they are relatively indifferent to its intellectual demands. The *vocational* culture is similarly anti-intellectual, but students do not identify with the college as a social object either; it is primarily

---

5. C. R. Pace, "Differences in Campus Atmosphere," in W. W. Charters, Jr., and N. L. Gage, eds., *Readings in the Social Psychology of Education* (Boston: Allyn & Bacon, 1963), p. 75.

6. *Ibid.*

7. Trow, *op. cit.*, pp. 205–07.

viewed only as an adjunct to the world of jobs. Emphasis here is on earning a degree that will help in getting a good job. As Trow succinctly puts it: "If the symbol of the collegiate culture is the football and fraternity weekend, the symbol of the vocationally oriented college culture is the student placement office."

The distinctive feature of the *academic culture* is its identification with the serious intellectual concerns of the faculty. The symbols of this culture are the library and the laboratory. The *nonconformist* culture is similar to the academic culture in its emphasis on ideas, but it is relatively detached from the intellectual emphasis of the faculty and more in tune with off-campus intellectual currents. As Trow remarks, "The distinctive quality of this student style is a rather aggressive nonconformism, a critical detachment from the college and its faculty (though this often conceals a strong ambivalence) and a general hostility to the college administration."

As might be anticipated from the interschool differences described earlier, these subcultures delineated by Trow are present in varying degrees and combinations on most campuses. According to him, the Berkeley campus of the University of California, though sharing in all these cultures, is predominantly collegiate. At San Francisco State College the collegiate culture is largely absent, with the academic and nonconformist cultures similarly weak; the predominant culture is the vocational. In contrast, Reed and Swarthmore colleges are heavily academic in subcultural orientation, with some emphasis on nonconformity. Both the vocational and collegiate cultures are weak in these two institutions.

The contrast between intellectual values at different colleges was analyzed in a study of 33,982 college students in 135 American colleges and universities.[8] Students were asked to indicate which of four purposes or results of college were most important. These included "A basic general education and appreciation of ideas," "Having a good time while getting a degree," "Career training," and "Developing the ability to get along with different kinds of people." While in practically all schools the majority of students chose the first alternative, the proportion of students selecting intellectualism varied considerably from school to school.

High school climates also vary. One study indicated this by

---

8. Davis, *op. cit.,* p. 114.

asking boys in ten high schools to rank from one to six the following alternatives to the question, "What does it take to get to be important and looked up to by the other fellows here at school?" [9]

> Coming from the right family
> Leader in activities
> Having a nice car
> High grades, honor roll
> Being an athletic star
> Being in the leading crowd

Girls were asked a similar question, with "clothes" and "Being a cheer leader," substituted for "Having a nice car" and "Being an athletic star" on their list of alternatives. The responses seemed to reveal differences in the value climates of the ten schools. To illustrate, although the item "High grades, honor roll" was ranked relatively low by students in all schools, standing fourth out of six for the boys and fifth out of six for the girls, its position varied considerably from school to school. For example, grades were ranked relatively high in a parochial high school for boys located in a large, urban area where the student body was largely lower-middle-class and of foreign-born or second-generation parentage. Surprisingly, this item was ranked relatively low in an upper-middle-class, suburban high school.

Up to this point we have been discussing campus climates as if they affected all participants equally. But this is obviously not true. For reasons of social background and personality, an individual will accept some campus values to a greater extent than others. Moreover, the broad campus climates we have discussed are differentiated further by various campus subgroups, and a student is most apt to be influenced by the values of the subgroups to which he belongs. For example, sorority women stress social skills and academic achievement to a greater extent than independent women students. Fraternity men do not differ from independent men in these characteristics, but they are lower than independents in intellectualism. [10]

Not only do the values emphasized on a campus vary according to the subgroup that is identified, but the pressures a student is exposed to vary with the position he occupies. A student is not

---

9. J. S. Coleman, *The Adolescent Society* (New York: Macmillan, 1961).
10. W. A. Scott, *Values and Organizations: A Study of Fraternities and Sororities* (Chicago: Rand McNally, 1965).

subjected to the same pressures throughout his four years in college. The social forces acting on a freshman are apt to be quite different from those acting upon him when he becomes a senior. The importance of position within the overall social structure of the institution is shown clearly by a study of 1,772 students who were followed from the beginning to the end of their college training.[11] Pressures from faculty and students were found to be quite different for upperclassmen than for lowerclassmen. For example, upperclassmen perceived strong pressures from the faculty toward high academic performance and independent thinking; lowerclassmen did not. Also, lowerclassmen perceived intense competition from other students for high achievement; upperclassmen did not.

CONSEQUENCES OF VARIOUS INSTITUTIONAL CLIMATES

School climates have consequences for student performance. An attempt to demonstrate this has been provided in a study of the degree to which college climates motivate their graduates to pursue Ph.D. degrees.[12] This study incorporates a number of improvements over previous ones. One common problem has been that schools differ in the proportion of talented students they attract; thus it has been difficult to determine whether student achievements at a particular school were due to the proportion of good students or to the social climate of the institution, or both. Here an attempt was made to assess the influence of an institution alone on aspirations to obtain a Ph.D. and to obtain results that would be uncontaminated by the proportion of entering students with high aspirations. The number of students from each school intending to obtain a Ph.D. was adjusted according to the proportion of talented students attending each school. Thus, the question to be answered was whether a school influenced students to pursue advanced degrees in proportion to the ability of its entering students or whether it led disproportionately few or many students to pursue a Ph.D.

The same study also used a refined version of the College Characteristics Inventory, which measured separately the influence of the faculty and of the students.

---

11. D. L. Thistlethwaite and N. Wheeler, "Effects of Teacher and Peer Subcultures upon Student Aspirations," *Journal of Educational Psychology*, Vol. 57 (1966), pp. 35–47.
12. Thistlethwaite, *op. cit.*

One finding was that, although some characteristics of the school climate were associated with productivity of a large number of Ph.D.-oriented graduates in all fields, certain characteristics—particularly of the faculty—were associated with high productivity of graduates who later received doctorates in the natural sciences. Faculty characteristics associated with motivating students to obtain Ph.D.'s in the arts, humanities, and social sciences differed in part. Both faculties were perceived by students as warm and informal in their relationships with students. Natural science faculty were relatively nondirective in their teaching methods. Faculties in the humanities and the social sciences displayed energy and controversy in instruction and flexibility of curriculum.

Student cultures also differed. Ph.D. candidates in the humanities were most often from schools where the student culture valued poetry, music, painting, sculpture, and similar activities, where broad interests were supported by round-table or panel discussions, and where an interest in ideas and reflection was evident in capacity attendance at lectures by outstanding visitors. They were seldom the product of schools where student social functions were highly valued and such practices as hazing and teasing were common. Student cultures where science was a common topic of discussion and highly valued were more productive of future Ph.D.'s in the natural sciences. Those stressing social conformity were low in this respect. Whether these prevailing campus climates changed the aspirations of the entering student toward graduate school is not clear from these data alone. This question is answered in the study described below.

This study used another method for controlling the effects of the proportion of talented students enrolled at a college.[13] Only those students who had raised or lowered their graduate school aspirations *after* entering college were considered. All those whose plans had remained unchanged by their college experiences were omitted from the sample. Student climate had little relation to the students' Ph.D. aspirations. As in the previous investigation, however, faculty orientation was important. Where the faculty was enthusiastic and emphasized achievement, humanism, and independence, the schools' productivity of Ph.D.'s was high. Schools where

---

13. D. L. Thistlethwaite, "College Press and Changes in Study Plans of Talented Students," *Journal of Educational Psychology*, Vol. 51 (1960), pp. 222–34.

the faculty lacked these attributes and emphasized compliance and conformity had less than their share of Ph.D. aspirants. In this investigation, the negative finding for the student climate was attributed to the fact that all the subjects were winners or near-winners of National Merit Scholarships, individuals less likely than the average college student to be influenced by the student climate.

High school climates appear to be similarly related to motivation to attend college. A review of four studies of variations between high schools in student plans to attend college confirms this.[14] Similar support comes from comparing the effects of school climate, social class, and ability on plans to attend college.[15] School climate was indexed on the basis of the proportion of students from families of various social classes. In predicting which students would attend college, ability and social class background appeared to be equally important, and the social climate of the high school less so. The predictive value of the first two variables appeared to be affected by the third. In those high schools having a climate most favorable to college attendance both ability and social-class background were more predictive of a senior's educational future, with ability accounting for the greater part of the variation. In the least favorable climate, social class was the most reliable predictor of college attendance.

While much research on school climates has focused on their effect on aspirations for further education, other consequences have also been examined. Where the high school climate stressed academic excellence, intellectual ability and grades were more strongly related, especially among above-average students. Where this climate was lacking, these students were less apt to perform according to their abilities. While not nearly as important as family background, school climate did have some relation, particularly for girls, to the amount of time spent studying and on the intention

---

14. R. P. Boyle, "The Effect of the High School on Students' Aspirations," *American Journal of Sociology*, Vol. 71 (1966), pp. 628–39. The four studies reviewed are: A. B. Wilson, "Residential Segregation of Social Classes and Aspirations of High School Boys," *American Sociological Review*, Vol. 24 (1959), pp. 836–45; N. R. Ramsy, *American High School at Mid-Century* (New York: Bureau of Applied Social Research, Columbia University, 1961); Coleman, *op. cit.*; R. H. Turner, *The Social Context of Ambition* (San Francisco: Chandler, 1964).

15. J. A. Michael, "High School Climates and Plans for Entering College," *Public Opinion Quarterly*, Vol. 25 (1961), pp. 585–95.

to go to college. Finally, in those schools where the value climate favored the all-round boy, the top scholars and the top athletes had the least grade difference. Where the school climate favored the specialist—where more students were named as either a scholar or an athlete but not as both—the grade difference between the scholars and athletes was greatest.[16]

SOURCES OF DIFFERENCES BETWEEN CAMPUS CLIMATES

A variety of institutional characteristics have been associated with variations in institutional climates. A sample of students in 135 American colleges and universities showed that college climates emphasizing intellectualism were more typical of small, private, high-quality institutions than of large, less selective, public institutions.[17] Correlations have been reported between college characteristics and various clusters of scores on the College Characteristics Index.[18] For example, those schools having a high ratio of library volumes to enrollment, a high percentage of Ph.D.'s on the faculty, and a high percentage of seniors in liberal-arts courses were more apt to have climates emphasizing humanism and intellectualism. Institutional climates stressing social status and a practical orientation were more apt to have fraternities and sororities. Community colleges are more likely to have a vocational climate than are universities.[19] These institutional characteristics, such as the quality of library facilities, faculty, and entering students are relatively enduring characteristics of a college or university and are often sufficient to establish a social climate emphasizing intellectual or academic values.

Various characteristics of high schools that may affect climate have also been studied. One study, comparing 13 high schools of varying size, suggested that the smaller schools evoked more varied extracurricular activities, more active involvement, and more chances for responsible leadership.[20] One study of high school size

---

16. Coleman, *op. cit.*
17. Davis, *op. cit.*
18. Pace, *op. cit.*
19. P. S. Campbell, "Personality Needs of Community College and University Students and Their Perceptions of the Press of Their Institutions: An Experimental Investigation," *Dissertation Abstracts*, Vol. 25, No. 4 (1964), p. 2603.
20. R. G. Barker and P. V. Gump, *Big School, Small School: High School Size and Student Behavior* (Stanford: Stanford University Press, 1964), p. 250.

in Kentucky indicated that pupils from larger schools outperform
those from smaller schools on standardized achievement tests; [21]
however, another study of academic achievement of students compared according to high school of origin reported no difference between students from small and large schools.[22]

Parochial and public schools have been compared in a number of studies. Children from higher-income, white-collar, and bet-
ter-educated families in metropolitan areas are more likely to attend parochial schools than those with a different family background.[23] One study reports that parochial school students perform
better than public school students on achievement tests, when
matched for sex and geographic region.[24] That the religious orientation of the school has some effect on education is shown in a
study which reports that Catholic parochial school students compare unfavorably with Protestants, Jews, and Catholic students in
public schools on a test of open-mindedness.[25]

Three factors possibly contributing to the social climate of an
educational institution are: (1) the attributes that entering students
bring with them, (2) the characteristics of the institution itself, and
(3) the informal social structures and cultural elements passed from
one generation of students to another. These three factors are not
independent of each other, but interact to some extent. For example, the quality of the entering students is dependent on the
characteristics of the institution itself. First, the kinds of students
who enroll vary greatly from school to school because of selective
admission policies. Colleges and universities varying in degree programs offered, size, location, tuition charges, and admission policies are apt to have student bodies that differ initially in abilities,
values, and motives by virtue of family, residential, and social class
backgrounds. Similarly, public schools on both elementary and sec-

21. P. Street, J. H. Powell, and J. W. Hamblem, "Achievement of Students and
    Size of School," *Journal of Educational Research*, Vol. 55 (1962), pp. 261–65.
22. E. R. Altman, "The Effect of Rank in Class and Size of High School on
    Academic Achievement of Central Michigan College, Class of 1957," *Journal
    of Educational Research*, Vol. 52 (1959), pp. 307–09.
23. A. M. Greeley and P. H. Rossi, "Correlates of Parochial School Attendance,"
    School Review, Vol. 72, No. 1 (1964), pp. 52–73.
24. R. H. Bauerfeind and W. S. Blumenfeld, "A Comparison of Achievement
    Scores of Public School and Catholic School Pupils," *Educational and Psycho-
    logical Measurements*, Vol. 23 (1963), pp. 331–36.
25. P. V. Quinn, "Critical Thinking and Openmindedness in Pupils from Pub-
    lic and Catholic Secondary Schools," *Journal of Psychology*, Vol. 66, No. 1
    (1965), pp. 23–30.

ondary levels, because they serve children of a given residential area, differ markedly from one another in student body composition with respect to race, social class, and other characteristics related to ability, values, and motives. Such student characteristics naturally have profound effects on the kind of climate prevailing in an institution.

A second source of variation in climate stems from the influence of the formal structure of the school, its administrative policies, its curriculum, the quality of its faculty, and so on, as these factors directly affect the climate itself. Schools on both the college and precollege levels vary markedly in these respects. Finally, many schools have traditions with respect to both academic and social activities that are sustained over a long period of time. New students are socialized by the older ones to adopt the prevailing values and norms.

While attempts have been made to determine the relative importance of these three sources of influence, it is difficult to draw any firm conclusions. One series of articles reflects a controversy over how data are to be interpreted.[26] While the more technical aspects of the discussion are beyond the scope of this book, several reasons can be offered in simpler language to explain some of the difficulty. First, on the basis of the data that are usually collected, it is extremely difficult to identify the separate contribution of each of the three factors to the social climate of the institution or to academic performance and aspirations. Data are typically measured at one point in time rather than longitudinally and often consist of rather crude indices. The correlational analysis resulting from such data rarely permits the identification of causal factors. Ability as measured by performance tests, for instance, is generally

---

26. D. L. Thistlethwaite, "College Environments and the Development of Talent," *Science*, Vol. 130 (1959), pp. 71–76; A. W. Astin, "A Re-examination of College Productivity," *Journal of Educational Psychology*, Vol. 52, No. 3 (1961), pp. 173–78; "Influences on the Student's Motivation to Seek Advanced Training: Another Look," *Journal of Educational Psychology*, Vol. 53 (1962), pp. 303–09; Astin and Holland, *op. cit.*; Astin, "An Empirical Characterization of Higher Educational Institutions," "Influences on the Student's Motivation to Seek Advanced Training: Another Look," 1962; "Differential College Effects on the Motivation of Talented Students to Obtain the Ph.D.," *Journal of Educational Psychology*, Vol. 54, No. 1 (1963), pp. 63–71; "Further Validation of the Environmental Assessment Technique," *Journal of Educational Psychology*, Vol. 54, No. 4 (1963), pp. 217–26; D. L. Thistlethwaite, "Fields of Study and Development of Motivation to Seek Advanced Training," *Journal of Educational Psychology*, Vol. 53 (1962), pp. 53–64.

thought of as something that the student brings into the situation; yet, scores on such tests are undoubtedly influenced by curriculum and by peer-group variables. The influence of the college press stemming from the faculty and the curriculum is frequently not separated from that stemming from the peer group. When separate indices of these pressures have been obtained, they generally have been assessed through the perceptions of the students, a procedure that raises questions as to their independence. We mean here that the actual pressures exerted by the faculty may be quite different from those pressures as seen through the students' eyes. Their report of faculty pressures may be contaminated with other pressures emanating from student sources.

We have already noted that the various environmental pressures do not affect all students equally; thus, precise research calls for quantitative assessment of the nature and strength of each aspect of the social climate and the numbers of students affected by it. But this ideal is a long way from realization.

Finally, what evidence there is suggests that the effect of any one factor is often modified by the presence of other factors, producing so-called *interaction effects*. When many factors must be considered simultaneously, interactions among them are extremely difficult to interpret. For instance, an examination of four studies which compared the influence of the family with that of the high school on student aspirations showed that the relative influence of the two depended on the size of the school, the sex of the student, and the size of the community.[27] In large cities, the effect of the high school was roughly equal to that of the family, but in small communities it was weaker. Regardless of community size, the high school was slightly less important for girls. Another example is provided by a significant finding of an extensive study on the effects of the racial composition of schools: the influence of the school was shown to depend on the quality of the family influences.[28] When a child from a family background which was supportive of his educational efforts was placed in a school where most pupils came from homes providing only weak support, his performance was little different from the performance of children like himself placed with children also from homes with strong educational support. More-

27. Boyle, *op. cit.*
28. J. S. Coleman, E. Q. Campbell, C. J. Hobson, *et al., Equality of Educational Opportunity* (Washington, D.C.: U.S. Office of Education, 1966).

over, when a child from a home background lacking in educational strength was placed with schoolmates who had strong supportive backgrounds, his achievement increased.

Despite the difficulties of interpreting findings, the class of variables generally thought to determine most strongly the school climate are the characteristics that the students bring to the school —their abilities, interests, and values as determined by influences outside the school. In the remainder of this chapter, however, we will be concerned with the influence on climate contributed by the formal and informal structure of the school. These structures offer the greatest potential for deliberate change for the advancement of educational aims. Except for the private sector of the educational system, the input characteristics of students are largely beyond the effective control of the educator, and even in that sector there are limits, particularly for the classroom teacher. Of the two remaining sources, we will concentrate on the informal structure, dealing with the formal structure largely in terms of its influence on the peer group and its effectiveness in fostering educational objectives.

EFFECTS OF THE SOCIAL STRUCTURE OF THE INSTITUTION

The influence of the peer group on academic performance has been widely viewed as largely negative, despite evidence that peer-group values generally favor doing well in school. A study of high schools in Los Angeles reports that students who see others as a friend, "a wheel," or "a brain," are apt to apply to a person two or three of these characterizations simultaneously. This suggests that those who do well in school are not only liked but also are accorded positions of status and influence.[29] Negative influences of the peer group are suggested by studies which confront adolescents with choices that reflect the degree to which they value educational goals relative to other goals. Of these studies, one has been most influential.[30] Boys in 10 Midwestern high schools were asked to indicate which of four things they wanted to be: a jet pilot, a nationally famous athlete, a missionary, or an atomic scientist. "Scientist" was selected by 25 percent of those answering, as compared with 32 percent who chose "jet pilot" and 37 percent who chose "athlete." Girls chose the more

---

29. Turner, *op. cit.*
30. Coleman, *The Adolescent Society.*

glamorous occupations of model and nurse over the more academic occupation of schoolteacher. The students were also given a choice of three things that they would most like to be remembered as being: a brilliant student, most popular, and (for boys) an athletic star, or (for girls) a leader in activities. The athletic star was the choice of the largest group of boys (44 percent). "Brilliant student" was chosen less frequently (31 percent), and "most popular" was least frequently chosen (25 percent). For the girls, being remembered as "a leader in activities" and "most popular" were about equally valued, 36 and 35 percent choosing these alternatives over "the brilliant-student" option, which was favored by 25 percent.

Responses to the question, "What does it take to be in the leading crowd?" similarly revealed less emphasis on academic performance than on other criteria. Only 12 percent of the girls mentioned grades, being smart, or being intelligent. Girls more frequently mentioned having a nice personality, good looks, good clothes, and a good reputation, being friendly, dressing neatly, and having money. Boys mentioned good grades more frequently than girls, but academic achievement was still fifth in frequency, behind personality, good looks, good clothes, and a good reputation. Similar questions and a sociometric analysis supported the conclusion that the athlete and the leader in school activities is more highly esteemed than the scholar.

However, the comparative context of the questionnaire items here should be kept in mind.[31] These results do not demonstrate that academic achievement is negatively valued, and thus they do not contradict the results of other studies but show that, compared with some other values, good grades are less salient and positive. But the comparatively low value placed on academic achievement

---

31. Coleman's study has been criticized on several counts. For example, he offered the pupil a choice between the items: "breaking with a friend," and "gaining disapproval from parents." The former is worded so as to appear more undesirable; Epperson found that when the term "disapproval" is used in both items, only 20 percent of his subjects prefer to incur the disapproval of their parents, compared with 43 percent in the Coleman study (D. C. Epperson, "A Re-assessment of Indices of Parental Influence in The Adolescent Society," *American Sociological Review*, Vol. 29 (1964), pp. 93–96). Other reviewers have questioned the existence of a distinct adolescent subculture as described by Coleman: C. W. Gordon, "Essay Review: James Coleman on 'The Adolescent Society,'" *School Review*, Vol. 25 (1963), pp. 377–85; M. Jahoda and N. Warren, "The Myths of Youth," *Sociology of Education*, Vol. 38 (1965), pp. 138–49.

by the peer group is apt to render ineffective the upward pressures on educational aspiration stemming from parents and other adults.

Two pieces of evidence from the study support this. First, parents had higher educational aspirations for their children than the children had for themselves. They much more frequently preferred their boys to be remembered as brilliant students rather than as athletic stars. Second, the attractiveness of the brilliant-student image compared to that of the athletic star varied at different times of the school year. In particular, during the freshman and sophomore years the attractiveness of the brilliant-scholar image is stronger in the fall of the year than in the spring. What is suggested here is that home influences send the student to school in the fall with higher educational aspirations, which diminish during the school year as he comes under the influence of the peer-group culture.

A similar picture emerges at the college level. A study of the student culture of a small, Midwestern college found that freshmen who initially valued grades moved toward the less academic norms of the upperclassmen during the course of the school year.[32]

The reason for preferring athletic prowess to academic achievement may be that athletic victories bring glory and consequent rewards of increased status to all students and to members of the community at large.[33] This is particularly the case in smaller communities where high school competition is a focus of intercommunity rivalry. In contrast, the victories of the scholar are personal ones gained at the expense of classmates who have to work harder to keep up.

As discussed in more detail in Chapter Five, social pressures restricting performance more often develop for academic achievement than athletic competition. This follows from a social psychological principle governing the choice of persons for comparison. Persons most often compare themselves with others who are similar to rather than different from themselves. In the case of abilities they compare themselves with persons whose ability level is perceived to be near their own, but not with those who are obviously superior or inferior. The cues to differences in physical ability are obvious. Star athletes are recognized as clearly superior in physical

32. W. L. Wallace, *Student Culture* (Chicago: Aldine, 1966).
33. Coleman, *The Adolescent Society*.

endowments, and a poor athletic performance is not experienced as disgraceful because we do not compare ourselves with the athlete. But the cues to mental ability are unclear; we do compare ourselves with the better students because we do not perceive them as so different from us. Along with the fact that athletic competition pits team against team rather than individual against individual, with the rewards going to the team and, vicariously at least, to many others, this probably accounts for the partly negative image of the brilliant scholar and the almost wholly positive image of the star athlete.

Further evidence consistent with the idea that competition for grades may be particularly bruising comes from a study of high school rebellion.[34] The most rebellious pupils were middle-class boys who were failing in school. In comparison to lower-class boys, they had internalized to a greater degree the middle-class goal of success in school; hence, failure in academic competition was more likely to arouse shame and guilt. Lower-class boys are less apt to accept educational goals, and their failure to achieve them would be less disturbing.

Sources of boredom and rebellion in the high school classroom were also revealed. Such behavior has been termed *expressive alienation,* which is characterized by (a) short-run hedonism, (b) negativism with respect to conformity and those who conform, (c) the perception of the status system as unfair, particularly as administered by the school authorities, and (d) demands for autonomy and freedom from adult interference. This psychological state may arise from an inability to meet school demands, as in the case of the rebellious middle-class boys; or, in the case of other students, it may arise from a lack of articulation between school activity and future status. For those students whose class, racial, or ethnic background, or intelligence, leads to the expectation that they will not achieve the desired level of occupational status under any circumstances, achievement in school makes little sense. Grades and other indicators of successful progress toward desirable adult status have little meaning. In the search for other symbols which provide assurance of growing up, these children prematurely demand adult status and reject the cultural doctrine that authority should reside in adults. To the degree that the disadvantaged child has in-

---

34. A. L. Stinchcombe, *Rebellion in a High School* (Chicago: Quadrangle Books, 1964).

ternalized success goals, he will evidence rebellion. The study concludes:

> The major practical conclusion of the analysis above is that rebellious behavior is largely a reaction to the school itself and to its promises, not a failure of the family or community. High school students can be motivated to conform by paying them in the realistic coin of future adult advantages. Except perhaps for pathological cases, any student can be made to conform if the school can realistically promise something valuable to him as a reward for working hard. But for a large part of the population, especially the adolescents who will enter the male working class or the female candidates for early marriage, the school has nothing to promise.[35]

This line of reasoning was not only supported by the data from this study but also is consistent with other studies showing high rates of rebellion among lower-class boys, girls oriented largely to the marriage market rather than the labor market, and students experiencing academic failure.

INFLUENCE PROCESSES IN INTERACTION

At a number of points in the preceding discussion we have noted that cultural influences do not uniformly affect all students in a given school. In part, this is due to the fact that the culture of a school is rarely homogeneous; rather, it consists of cultural strains or subcultures carried by subgroups of students as well as other institutional participants such as the faculty. In part, this occurs because students differ with respect to their chances of encountering, or having encountered, such influences and because they differ in their receptivity to such influences. In the remainder of this chapter we examine how subcultural influences are distributed.

The influence of a subculture on an individual's academic motivation and achievement depends on (1) the frequency of his contact with the group or groups mediating the influence, and (2) his receptivity to this influence once he encounters it. The effects of *frequency of interaction* and *receptivity* on educational aspirations and achievement can best be understood by thinking of these interactions as an exchange of rewards and costs.

This "exchange theory" suggests that the attraction which one

---

35. A. L. Stinchcombe, *Rebellion in a High School* (Chicago: Quadrangle Books, 1964), p. 179.

person has for another depends upon the extent to which the *rewards* minus the *costs* experienced in interaction with the other person exceed the individual's *comparison level*.[36] The term *reward* refers to any consequence of interaction that gratifies a need. The term *cost* is similarly broadly conceived to include consequences of interaction that frustrate needs, including such *costs* as fatigue, anxiety, or embarrassment. The term *comparison level* refers to that point on a scale of outcomes above which the person experiences pleasure and satisfaction, and below which he experiences displeasure or dissatisfaction. The comparison level for an individual is influenced by his past outcomes, by what he perceives other persons like him to be receiving, by what he could obtain in alternative relations, and by several other factors.

An individual's attraction to a group can be a powerful source of influence. If the group in question is a major source of rewards, if it functions to minimize costs, and if the individual does not have alternative sources providing similar outcomes, the group has great power over his behavior.

This proposition has received considerable support in a variety of contexts. For example, in the study of the culture at a small, Midwestern college previously referred to, those students with the greatest desire to be accepted and liked by their fellow students experienced the greatest shift downward in their orientation toward grades.[37] Further, downward effects were generally accentuated for those students choosing to join fraternities and sororities, where fellow members were more apt to hold norms and values less favorable to academic achievement. At the same time this downward direction was generally reduced, and in some instances reversed, for those students most attracted to the faculty, whose orientation favored academic excellence.

Factors influencing both frequency of interaction and consequent reward-cost outcomes and the perception of alternative sources of interaction which contribute to comparison level may be classified as external or internal. Examples of external characteristics are physical and institutional arrangements; examples of internal characteristics are attitudes, values, and self concepts. Physical arrangements may directly prevent or enforce interaction, or they may

36. H. H. Kelley and J. W. Thibaut, *The Social Psychology of Groups* (New York: Wiley, 1959).
37. Wallace, *op. cit.*

in varying degrees discourage or encourage interaction through their influence on costs and rewards. For instance, other things being equal, it is less costly to interact with those who are physically close than with those who are distant. The elementary and secondary school attended depends on one's area of residence. This excludes as possible school associates children living in other areas. Within a given school, grouping by multiple sections of the same class, by ability, by a differentiated curriculum at the high school level, and so on, all serve to encourage higher rates of interaction among some children to the exclusion of others. On the college level, course scheduling, living and eating arrangements, workload pressures, and various geographic and architectural features may similarly channel interaction. One would expect to find more frequent contacts between those in the same major fields or those in the same dormitory. These external features are particularly important in determining patterns of association during initial phases of group formation; they serve as limiting factors to the range of acquaintanceship because they prevent purely random sampling of the outcomes to be experienced in all possible relations between members of a given population.

Support for the initial importance of these factors in an educational setting is found in a study of acquaintanceship among housemates on a university campus.[38] Early in the history of this group, more close relations developed between students on the same floor than between those on different floors. As might be expected, roommates were particularly prone to mutual attraction during this phase of acquaintanceship. This also explains the somewhat puzzling finding in another study that friendship choices among medical students were related to the proximity of their names in alphabetical listings.[39] This apparently was a result of grouping students for lectures and laboratory assignments in alphabetical order.

In time, however, the patterns dictated exclusively by these external factors give way to a variety of internal variables. The needs, attitudes and values, and self concepts of persons encountering each other are such as to make some interactions more rewarding and less costly. Such interactions then begin to exclude others.

38. T. M. Newcomb, *The Acquaintance Process* (New York: Holt, Rinehart and Winston, 1961).
39. Patricia Kendall, "Medical Education as Social Process," paper read at American Sociological Association, New York, August 1960.

Individuals find rewarding interaction with persons who provide support for their existing needs, attitude and value structures, and particularly their self concepts. This has generally been reflected in studies showing that persons seek out others who have similar attitudes toward objects of importance, such as self and others. Thus, among the campus housemates mentioned earlier, the friendship patterns that *finally* prevailed were those in which students preferring each other held similar values. Friends also held similar opinions about various other house members, especially about each other. In both experimental and field studies, persons tend to like and associate with others who see them as they see themselves and who allow them to behave in a manner consistent with their self concepts.[40]

To the extent that this tendency influences the frequency of association and the degree of attraction between persons, it seems to maintain stability and discourage change. The student who has a positive attitude toward academic achievement and who sees himself as a good student is likely to seek out others who have similar values and who confirm his identity as a serious student.

For the most part these factors affecting exposure and receptivity to social influence in the school situation play a conservative role; they often subject the student to influences that will maintain stability rather than induce change. This should explain, in part at least, the importance of the personal and social-background characteristics that students bring with them into the educational situation. The child of a particular family and class will go to school with children of similar backgrounds because of the homogeneity of most school districts. Even where the school does include children from different backgrounds, as sometimes occurs in elementary schools and more frequently in secondary schools, the effects of ability grouping in the former and differences in curriculum in the latter—those intending to go to college take different courses from those with commercial or vocational goals—minimize exposure to opposing influences. Add to this the tendency for persons to choose as friends those with similar interests, abilities, and social-background characteristics, and it is easy to understand that the informal structure of the school, the extracurricular organization, and the

---

40. P. F. Secord and C. W. Backman, "An Interpersonal Approach to Personality," in Brendan Maher, ed., *Progress in Experimental Personality Research* (New York: Academic Press, 1965).

cliques or friendship groups subject their members to cultural influences that work in the direction of stability rather than change.

Under certain circumstances, however, the school climate may have a greater effect than our previous discussion has suggested. This is apt to occur where the character and the climate of the school are markedly at variance with student characteristics and family background. The lower-class child, white or Negro, in a predominantly middle-class school, or the adolescent from a politically conservative home who enters a school with a liberal political ethos, are cases in point. In both instances they appear to be markedly influenced by their new school environment. Sometimes the individual's own characteristics, particularly his attitudes and self concept, are inadequately anchored in nonschool groups. In this instance he is apt to find support in the various school groups. Our previous discussion has suggested yet another set of circumstances. To the extent that the individual is confronted with a homogeneous climate which prevents the process of selectivity from operating, it should be more influential. Obviously, if the institution contains many subcultures, with widely varying values, it becomes easy for the student to affiliate with groups whose values are at variance with the values of the faculty or even with the overall school climate. Thus, the small college is more effective in socializing its members than the large university.[41]

Implications for the Classroom

Where the student and others about him, particularly his peers, value academic excellence, successful performance in the classroom is likely to be encouraged by self-approval and the approval of other persons. But for the majority of students, academic values rank relatively low in the hierarchy of peer-group values. Athletics and social life take precedence in most schools.

The value structure of a school is in part a function of the values of the students and, to a lesser degree, the faculty, and in part it reflects the unique history of the school. This suggests that one method of affecting the value climate of a school is to con-

---

41. T. M. Newcomb, "Student Peer-Group Influence and Intellectual Outcomes of College Experience," in R. L. Sutherland *et al., op. cit.,* pp. 69–91.

trol the mix of input characteristics. The admission policies of institutions of higher education, as well as geographic districting of schools at the primary and secondary levels, combined with patterns of residential segregation by class, race, and ethnic origin, control the input of student characteristics in a given school. Unfortunately, particularly in the public schools, the mix is not controlled to optimize the educational benefits of the resultant school climate for all children. Resistance to outright or de facto segregation in the schools by consolidation, redistricting, and so on, prevent experimentation with a more optimal mix. Those who resist such moves do so on the supposition that benefit to the disadvantaged child will be outweighed by the loss suffered by the child from the more favored environment. The evidence from the recent U.S. Office of Education equality of opportunity study does not confirm these fears.[42] Whereas the child from a disadvantaged background benefits by attending a school where the students come from homes providing a favorable background, the child with a favorable background appears relatively unaffected when placed in a school where the children are largely drawn from disadvantaged backgrounds.

The value climate of schools might be altered in the direction of academic excellence if greater emphasis were placed on group competition, intramural as well as between schools.[43] Just as athletic competition has led to the emphasis on athletic prowess in the adolescent world, so competition between groups or individuals as group representatives could be expected to result in rewards being conferred for excellence in other areas. Such forms of competition between schools as team debates, music or drama contests, and science fairs have been suggested. More radical schemes could be adopted, such as the organization of students into study or project teams, where the brighter students could augment the instructional process by serving in that capacity themselves.

Two characteristics of this type of competition that distinguish it from forms of individual competition must be kept in mind. Here the individuals compete as representatives of the group rather than as individuals, and for successful performance

42. Coleman, Campbell, and Hobson, *et al., op. cit.*
43. Coleman, *The Adolescent Society.*

the rewards in terms of prizes, increased status, and so forth go to the group. Second, in some of these, at least, not only is there a diffusion of the rewards but of the responsibility of winning or losing as well. Where the competing units are teams the win or loss depends on the joint efforts of the members. Both of these features have the effect of reducing the likelihood that invidious comparisons between individuals will be made, a reaction which gives rise to forces in restraint of effort and increases the likelihood that individuals will reward each other to the degree that their efforts contribute to a successful outcome which they share as a group. At the same time, the brighter, more academically oriented students would receive recognition as leaders in group competition and would serve as models instead of rivals.

Chapter Four

Diverging Patterns
of Achievement

Previous chapters have examined influences on the performance of a student as they operate at a particular point in time, with little attention to their relative strength at different stages in the student's career. The discussion of family influences upon academic performance, for example, stressed the preschool period. Naturally these influences continue as long as a student remains in school, but their relative importance and also the manner in which they operate varies greatly at different educational levels. We shall now review the role of the student from the beginning to the end of his formal education, examining in some detail the many factors that turn him in one direction or another during this period. Our analysis will attempt to show how *expectations* for an occupational role affect the direction a student takes at many choice points in his movement through the educational system. Similarly, the nature of the school system at different levels, the values of the peer group, and the behavior of his teachers may be expected to affect the progress of the student.

THE INDIVIDUAL STUDENT

We may think of the individual child as gradually acquiring certain abilities, skills, habits, and attitudes that affect his school performance. These attributes are prerequisites for adequate school performance. They have been discussed at length in Chapter Two; our purpose here is to assess their relative importance in guiding the movement of the student through the various educational levels.

Since we no longer think of mental abilities as fixed endowments, but rather as a set of gradually acquired skills,[1] an initial

---

1. J. McV. Hunt, *Intelligence and Experience* (New York: Ronald Press, 1961).

poor start constitutes a handicap that may attenuate subsequent learning. Many studies support the conclusion that the pattern of academic achievement is set early and that few children improve once they make a poor start. It has been shown that groups of children matched in intelligence and socioeconomic status but differing in initial achievement grow further apart in performance year by year.[2] Another longitudinal study indicates that initial underachievers slip further in school performance from the first through the twelfth grades.[3] Still another study found a substantial correlation between the fourth-grade achievement and the college success of Iowa students.[4]

The most extensive study of educational achievement ever conducted in the United States, entitled "Equality of Educational Opportunity," further supports this conclusion in the case of disadvantaged children.[5] Negro pupils, for example, are roughly one standard deviation below white pupils from grade one through grade twelve. Individual differences within a grade are increasingly larger at higher grade levels; this means that, if achievement is represented in terms of grade-years, the gap between Negro and white children widens from grade to grade. For example, at grade six, Negroes in the metropolitan northeastern United States are approximately 1½ years behind the average white pupil. At grade nine, they are approximately 2¼ years behind, and at grade twelve, 3¼ years behind. Next to Negroes, other minority groups showing performance decrements in lesser degree are Puerto Ricans, Mexican-Americans, and American Indians. Oriental Americans are not deficient in performance.[6]

While these data show clearly the differences in performance, they do not, of course, provide reasons. Part of this increasingly poor performance in school is probably due to the poor start in the early grades caused by lack of preschool preparation in the home. Chil-

2. J. R. Vane, "Relation of Early School Achievement to High School Achievement When Race, Intelligence and Socioeconomic Factors Are Equated," *Psychology in the Schools*, Vol. 3 (1966), pp. 124–29.
3. M. C. Shaw and J. R. McCuen, "The Onset of Academic Underachievement in Bright Children," *Journal of Educational Psychology*, Vol. 51 (1960), pp. 103–09.
4. D. P. Scannell, "Prediction of College Success from Elementary and Secondary Performance," *Journal of Educational Psychology*, Vol. 51 (1960), pp. 130–35.
5. J. S. Coleman, E. Q. Campbell, C. J. Hobson, *et al.*, *Equality of Educational Opportunity* (Washington, D.C.: U.S. Office of Education, 1966).
6. *Ibid.*

dren from many homes simply have not acquired certain necessary skills by the time they enter the first grade. Since learning in successive grades is built upon what has been learned initially, this poor start can have a long-range effect.

In part, the failure of disadvantaged children to keep up appears to be due to the continuing influence of family background. Data from the equality of opportunity study are illuminating.[7] It has often been asserted that minority pupils do not *aspire* to achieve in school, do not *aspire* to a college education, or do not have *ambitions* for high-status occupations. For this reason, it has been suggested, they perform poorly in school. A 1964 study provides some support for the view that individuals from disadvantaged families have a low level of aspiration.[8] However, evidence has been presented indicating that Negroes and whites have equal aspirations but differ in their *expectations of realizing* these aspirations.[9]

Recent evidence from the equality of opportunity study also shows that Negroes do not have lower educational aspirations. As many Negro as white pupils report that they would do almost anything to stay in school. Among minority groups, only Puerto Ricans are less inclined than whites to remain in school. Further, a considerably higher proportion of Negroes than whites report that they want to be good students. Negroes also aspire as much as whites to education beyond high school, although often their choice is not of a four-year college, but a technical, nursing, or business school. These high educational aspirations are matched by high aspirations for occupational achievement. The largest category of occupation chosen by all groups is the professions—not a realistic aspiration for all students. Only about 13 percent of the total labor force is currently so employed. The bulk of these findings indicate quite clearly that the differences in performance among minority groups are not due to differences in aspirations.[10]

Another common thesis is that disadvantaged children have low self-esteem: they feel incapable of performing at a high level in

7. *Ibid.*

8. David Gottlieb, "Goal Aspirations and Goal Fulfillments: Differences Between Deprived and Affluent American Adolescents," *American Journal of Orthopsychiatry*, Vol. 34 (1964), pp. 934–41.

9. B. C. Rosen, "Family Structure and Achievement Motivation," *American Sociological Review*, Vol. 26 (1961), pp. 574–85.

10. Coleman, Campbell, Hobson, *et al., op. cit.*

school tasks and thus do not put much effort into them. There is some empirical support for this view.[11] Once again, however, the equality of opportunity study provides partly contrary evidence. Several questions were asked pertaining to the self concept. In general, average differences between Negroes and whites were *not* found, although other minority groups had less favorable evaluations of themselves.[12]

A third attitude to be considered is *fate control*. Individuals vary in the degree to which they feel they have control over their destiny. If a child believes that his environment is capricious, or random, or beyond his ability to change, he may conclude that attempts to affect it are not worthwhile and stop trying. This would seem to be a relevant variable, because minority groups do in fact have less control over their destinies.

A 1963 study indicated that lower-class children see themselves as more externally controlled and less capable of determining what will happen to them than middle-class children.[13] Poverty may produce a feeling of powerlessness that pervades much of the individual's activities.[14]

The equality of opportunity study measured fate control by the following three questions:

1. Agree or disagree: Good luck is more important than hard work for success.
2. Agree or disagree: Every time I try to get ahead, something or somebody stops me.
3. Agree or disagree: People like me don't have much of a chance to be successful in life.[15]

On all three items, Negro and other minority children showed a much lower sense of control over their environment than did whites. Thus it appears that home, neighborhood, and peers, if they are the major source of this notion of fate control, produce an

---

11. D. P. Ausubel and P. Ausubel, "Ego Development Among Segregated Negro Children," in A. H. Passow, ed., *Education in Depressed Areas* (New York: Teachers College Press, Columbia University, 1963), pp. 109–41.
12. Coleman, Campbell, Hobson, *et al., op. cit.*
13. E. S. Battle and J. B. Rotter, "Children's Feelings of Personal Control as Related to Social Class and Ethnic Group," *Journal of Personality*, Vol. 31 (1963), pp. 482–90.
14. W. C. Haggstrom, "The Power of the Poor," in F. Riesman, J. Cohen, and A. Pearl, eds., *Mental Health of the Poor* (New York: Macmillan, 1964), pp. 205–23.
15. Coleman, Campbell, Hobson, *et al., op. cit.*, p. 288.

orientation toward life among minority groups which is a strong handicap to educational achievement.[16]

SCHOOL CHARACTERISTICS
AND EDUCATIONAL ACHIEVEMENT

We have indicated that informal preschool training in the home is important in determining the start a child gets in the first grade and that the kind of start he makes may have a lasting effect on his performance. This suggests that the school often does not compensate for inadequacies of the home or of early training. Evidence discussed below indicates that this is indeed the case.

In part, of course, poor performance is perpetuated because the disadvantaged child is apt to attend a primary school where teaching competence is low and where a disproportionate amount of time is spent in disciplinary functions. Even more important is the presence in the school of peers who are disadvantaged themselves. The equality of opportunity study has shown that the single most important factor in the school setting is the educational background and aspirations of the other students. A child with a poor family background is unlikely to improve if placed in a school with peers similar to himself. If, however, he attends a school where other pupils have better backgrounds and higher aspirations, he is apt to improve markedly. This effect is less for white pupils than it is for all minority groups except Orientals. Furthermore, white pupils from homes that are strongly supportive of education but who attend a school where most pupils have lower abilities and aspirations nevertheless do as well as if they were surrounded by pupils like themselves.[17] These results are consistent with the generalization that family background supportive of educational achievement is a prime requisite for academic success, since both white and Oriental families share this characteristic. But, where it is lacking, attending a school where one's peers are academically oriented may serve as an adequate substitute.

By controlling statistically for socioeconomic background, researchers have been able to assess the independent effect of school *facilities* on performance. In general, the equality of opportunity study found that such characteristics as well-equipped laboratories and libraries produced relatively *little* improvement. Most of the

16. *Ibid.*
17. *Ibid.*

differences in student achievement from one school to another could be accounted for by socioeconomic background, regardless of facilities.[18] The significance of this finding is questionable, however, because in controlling for socioeconomic background the investigators necessarily limited their comparisons of schools to those that differed little in facilities. This happened because so often schools with good facilities are the same schools which have students from higher socioeconomic strata, and vice versa.

School facilities apparently have more effect on the achievement of minority pupils than on that of white pupils. Thus, in the southern United States, where Negroes often attend especially poor schools, variation in school characteristics accounts for a larger proportion of individual differences in pupil achievement than in other parts of the country. Another caution in interpreting these results is that pupil achievement is reported only in terms of standardized tests, and it is quite possible that school characteristics might differentially affect achievement measured in other ways.[19]

The *teacher* may also influence educational achievement of his pupils. In the equality of opportunity study, teacher competence was measured crudely by the teacher's own verbal-test score and by his educational background and that of his parents. Teacher "quality," in this sense, was found to have an appreciably greater effect on pupil achievement than school facilities. Moreover, this effect was intensified in the higher grades.[20]

Given the teacher's goal of imparting knowledge and producing intellectual competence in his pupils, it is almost inevitable that he would favor high achievers and look unfavorably on low achievers. Many observers have also pointed out that if he is from the middle class, he will be more receptive to behavior exhibited by middle-class children and less approving of behavior of lower-class children. This tendency is important because it discourages underprivileged children and accentuates their difficulties. A particularly well-designed study carried out in Britain confirms this tendency.[21]

---

18. *Ibid.*
19. *Ibid.*
20. *Ibid.*
21. D. McIntyre, A. Morrison, and J. Sutherland, "Social and Educational Variables Relating to Teacher's Assessments of Primary School Pupils," *British Journal of Educational Psychology*, Vol. 36, No. 3 (1966), pp. 272–79.

A statistical analysis of teachers' ratings of their pupils on 25 traits indicated that the consideration most important to them might generally be described as "being a good pupil." Emphasis was placed on trustworthiness, attentiveness, courtesy, pleasantness, and attainment in school subjects. A second consideration, much less prominent in the ratings, concerned sociability and leadership.

Separate analyses of the schools according to social class indicated some interesting differences in the way teachers in these schools assessed their pupils. Among boys, teachers in middle-class and mixed-social-class schools generally favored those who were pleasant and trustworthy; in suburban, working-class schools, those who were clever; and in urban, working-class schools, those who were attentive and hard-working. Girls were perceived in more stereotyped and less analytic fashion, and also more similarly no matter what the class level of the school. The "ideal" girl was much the same whatever the social-class background, while the "ideal boy" appeared to vary according to his social-class origins.

The age of the teacher is also related to the student traits stressed as desirable. Older teachers were more tough-minded and conservative; they stressed attainment and such associated traits as persistence and enthusiasm. Younger teachers stressed good behavior to a greater extent.[22]

Studies carried out in the United States yield similar conclusions, although, since in many instances the studies are less comprehensive and thorough than the investigation just described, their conclusions are much more tentative. One study, for example, indicated that lower-class pupils found middle-class teachers more difficult to understand than lower-class teachers.[23]

These variations in the way teachers perceive and treat pupils of different social-class origins generally reinforce the handicaps or benefits that the pupil derives from his class origins.[24] Pupils from the lower class are apt to be seen as less capable and those having a more

---

22. *Ibid.*
23. M. L. Jackson and F. F. Fuller, "Influence of Social Class on Students' Evaluations of Their Teachers," *Proceedings of the 74th Annual Convention of the American Psychological Association* (Washington, D.C.: American Psychological Association, 1966), pp. 269–70.
24. W. L. Warner, R. J. Havighurst, and M. B. Loeb, *Who Shall Be Educated?* (New York: Harper & Row, 1944); A. B. Hollingshead, *Elmtown's Youth* (New York: Wiley, 1949); C. W. Gordon, *The Social System of the High School* (New York: Macmillan, 1957).

advantageous home background as brighter. Moreover, if teachers have more favorable attitudes toward middle-class pupils because of a greater perceived pleasantness and cooperativeness, this in itself encourages them toward greater achievement and toward continuing education.

ABILITY GROUPING AND STREAMING

We have saved for a separate discussion one aspect of schools, namely, the various systems of grouping children according to their ability, especially in the primary grades.

Grouping is perhaps most widespread in Great Britain, where it is called "streaming," although most urban schools in the United States also exercise some form of grouping. In recent years, educators and behavorial scientists have been re-evaluating the effects of streaming, with more and more eivdence pointing toward unfavorable consequences of this practice. First, it is apparent that the decision to place a child in a particular ability group is based only partly on ability, and partly on social-class origins. In 140 British schools having two ability groups, three-quarters of the pupils having fathers in professional or managerial occupations were in the higher group, and only one-quarter in the lower group. Of those pupils whose fathers were unskilled manual laborers, only two-fifths were in the higher group, and three-fifths in the lower group. Similar social-class distinctions were found in over 400 other schools having three or four ability groups.[25]

Such placement is *not* in proportion to the abilities of pupils from families in each occupational category. One study found that 11 percent more middle-class children are allocated to the upper streams than would be expected from their measured ability at eight years of age, and 26 percent fewer are placed in the lower streams.[26] This undoubtedly underestimates the social-class bias, since test performance at age eight has probably been influenced by the two years already spent in a particular ability group. The same study also indicated a strong bias in placement as a result of preschool maternal care. Dirty, badly clothed children appear in

---

25. Brian Jackson, *Streaming: An Education System in Miniature* (London: Routledge & Kegan Paul, 1964).
26. J. W. B. Douglas, *The Home and the School* (London: MacGibbon & Kee, 1964).

the lower groups to a considerably greater extent than their test performance warrants.

Finally, British studies in particular show marked social-class differences in the number of dropouts and in the number of pupils who go on to the highly desirable "grammar" schools. In the upper-middle class there were fourteen pupils in grammar schools for every one in a technical school, whereas among the lower-class children of manual laborers, there were only two pupils in grammar schools for every one in a technical school. This distribution is, of course, considerably out of proportion to the differences in ability between the two classes as measured at the time of selection.[27] Similarly, the percentage of those having left school at fifteen years of age varies from 15 percent in upper-middle-class families to 77 percent among lower-class manual laborers, a difference that is not explained solely by the difference in ability.[28]

Once a child is placed in a particular ability classification, he is apt to remain there. On the basis of normal shifts in intelligence test scores, about 40 percent of the children in various groups ought to be transferred from one group to another.[29] But the *actual* rate of transfer ranges from 1 to 5 percent. Thus, once placed in a low-ability grouping, the educational opportunities of most children are apt to be permanently reduced.

Although it is true that types of grouping differ markedly in different school districts and thus have somewhat different effects, certain general conclusions can be drawn. One British study compares grouped and ungrouped primaries,[30] another covers a large number of British schools having streaming,[31] and an American study compares two systems of grouping (ability versus random with enrichment) in a school district in the United States.[32]

"Unsegregated" schools (those having random grouping) were not found to be disadvantageous to the superior pupils. Superior pupils in ungrouped or randomly grouped schools made about as much academic progress as their counterparts in streamed schools. In the United States, ability grouping did not seem to result in

27. *Ibid.*
28. *Ibid.*
29. Cited in Jackson, *op. cit.*
30. Jackson, *op. cit.*
31. Douglas, *op. cit.*
32. W. R. Borg, *Ability Grouping in the Public Schools* (Madison, Wis.: Dembar Educational Research Services, 1966).

greater achievement.[33] In the British studies, however, pupils of average and low ability made much greater gains when placed in the upper streams than they did in the lower ones. In schools where streaming was practiced, the gap between the ability groups in academic-achievement-test scores widened year by year. Such gaps were much smaller in ungrouped schools.

Ability grouping has consequences that extend far beyond academic achievement. Teachers in systems with streaming tend to develop more rigid opinions concerning individual differences in children; they divide children into types—the bright, the average, and the dull. Moreover, these are thought of as enduring attributes of the children, as immutable, unchangeable, unassailable. That these attitudes do much to make the prophecy implied by the initial placement come true is suggested by a study demonstrating that children of equal ability perform at different levels if their teachers are led to adopt different *expectations* for their performance.[34] A further consequence is that teachers of low-ability groups may feel that they too have been "grouped," thus lowering their morale and efficiency.[35]

The streaming process influences friendships and tightens the groups further, perhaps reinforcing the different performance levels. There is a considerable social difference between streamed and unstreamed schools. In unstreamed schools, children were more cooperative and helpful toward each other, while the streamed schools emphasized competition.[36] In the United States, the self concept of both the average and the slow pupil suffers markedly in schools where ability grouping is practiced. Pupils, especially girls, in randomly grouped classes had more favorable attitudes toward self than those in ability-grouped sections. They also had higher self-acceptance. In addition, there were fewer pupils in the randomly grouped classes who were designated social isolates on sociometric tests.[37]

33. J. H. Shores, "What Does Research Say About Ability Grouping by Classes?" *Illinois Education,* Vol. 53 (1964), pp. 169–72.
34. R. Rosenthal and L. Jacobson, "Teachers' Expectancies: Determinants of Pupils' IQ Gains," *Psychological Reports,* Vol. 19 (1966), pp. 115–18.
35. R. Tillman and J. H. Hull, "Is Ability Grouping Taking Schools in the Wrong Direction?" *Nation's Schools,* Vol. 73 (1964), pp. 70–71, 128–29.
36. Jackson, *op. cit.*
37. Borg, *op. cit.*

DIVERGENT PATHS

The directions taken by students become increasingly divergent as they move further through the educational system. In Britain, pupils in the upper streams of the primary grades move in greater numbers into the grammar school, the primary route to college and university training. Those in the lower streams, if they continue in school at all, go on to technical or secondary schools which feed only a small number of students into college or university training. Although there is more freedom of movement in the United States, student choices and the direction of counselors often send students into a noncollege-oriented curriculum in high school.[38] Not only does this leave them *unprepared* for college but it orients them away from college through informal associations with classmates not college-bound.

Most of the research on student role-allocation has been devoted to the two most divergent role choices: dropping out of high school before graduation and going on to college and graduate school. We will first discuss factors associated with dropping out of school before graduation from high school and then follow the college-bound student into college, where, once again, he may drop out before graduation or, at the other extreme, go on to postgraduate work and an advanced degree.

The high school dropout has become a problem of increasing concern, not because more pupils are leaving school before being graduated, but because the character of the labor market is changing. Automation and continued advances in technology require more trained workers and fewer untrained ones. In contrast to earlier times, there is little place today for the strong and willing, but untutored, laborer; thus, an ever-increasing proportion of the unemployed are nongraduates.

One study of dropouts stressed the failure of the family to function adequately as a primary group.[39] Contemporary sociologists identify three characteristics of the *primary group:* (a) relations that are personal rather than impersonal—that involve the whole person; (b) communication that is deep and extensive; and

38. A. Cicourel and J. L. Kitsuse, *Educational Decision-Makers* (New York: Bobbs-Merrill, 1963).
39. L. F. Cervantes, *The Dropout* (Ann Arbor: University of Michigan Press, 1965).

(c) the provision of satisfying, happy experiences.[40] Studies of drop-outs indicate that their families fail to meet all three of these criteria. In one study, four out of five dropouts stated that their families had little understanding of them, while four out of five students who had been graduated indicated that their families understood them. Dropouts have less respect for their families and are somewhat rebellious toward them. Similar sharp differences were found on interview questions pertaining to frequency of communication, and marked but less extreme differences were found in the extent to which the family provided happy and satisfying experiences.[41]

A further difference between the families of the graduate and the dropout lay in the friendship and kinship ties associated with the family. The families of graduates had more ties to relatives and neighbors than did families of dropouts; moreover, friends of the graduate were more often approved by his family than were friends of the dropout. This condition can result in reinforcement of educational and other widely accepted values and thus help keep the student in school.[42]

A study comparing the attitudes held by parents of students who dropped out with parents of those who did not, matched on socioeconomic background, further documents these points. Mothers of students who stayed in school more often encouraged their children's schooling and were acquainted with families whose children attended college.[43]

Although the thesis that "the young culture" is cut off from the mainstream of society has strong support from many sociologists, the degree of this isolation apparently differs markedly between graduates and dropouts. Families of graduates were seen as maintaining considerable influence over them and, in fact, as being in agreement with them on many issues. Dropouts isolated themselves to a greater extent. They chose friends in defiance of their families' wishes and in many instances engaged in open rebellion against their families.[44] As might be expected, dropouts are usually found to be strongly antagonistic toward school authorities and

40. L. Broom and P. Selznick, *Sociology: A Text with Adapted Readings,* 2nd ed. (New York: Harper & Row, 1958).
41. Cervantes, *op. cit.*
42. *Ibid.*
43. F. V. Mannino, "Family Factors Related to School Persistence," *Journal of Educational Sociology,* Vol. 35 (1962), pp. 193–202.
44. Cervantes, *op. cit.*

their teachers. Unlike those who eventually graduate, they have little regard for them and little respect for their opinions. They much
prefer to consult their peers for advice—peers who themselves are
oriented away from school.[45]

Turning to the question of which students are college-bound,
we refer back to Chapter One, where we showed that family attitudes toward a college education and the family's occupational
aspirations for the child have some relation to whether a student
eventually goes to college. This is true whether families are classified according to socioeconomic level or more direct information
is obtained about their attitudes and behavior toward the education
of their children. In the present chapter, we have already reviewed
the effects of preschool experience in the family, early experience
in the primary grades, and ability grouping. As we have noted,
these earlier stages in the career of a pupil may have important
consequences for his later education.

An additional influence stems from the impact of high school
peers on an individual's decision to go to college. A variety of
studies support the view that peers influence a high school student's orientation toward or away from college.[46] Evidence in one
study indicates that peer-group status as a factor in college choice
increases markedly during the four years of high school.[47] Peer-
group status was defined in terms of membership in "the leading
crowd." A student was regarded as being a member of the leading
crowd if two or more students identified him as such in a questionnaire. Among high school freshmen, the intention of going to
college is more strongly associated with their father's educational
level and their parents' desire for them to attend college than with
belonging to the leading crowd. Among seniors, however, being a

45. *Ibid.*
46. A. O. Haller and C. E. Butterworth, "Peer Influences on Levels of Occupational and Educational Aspirations," *Social Forces,* Vol. 38 (1960), pp. 289–
95; E. L. McDill and J. S. Coleman, "High School Social Status, College
Plans, and Interest in Academic Achievement: A Panel Analysis," *American
Sociological Review,* Vol. 28, No. 6 (1963), pp. 905–18; C. N. Alexander, Jr.,
and E. Q. Campbell, "Peer Influences on Adolescent Educational Aspirations
and Attainments," *American Sociological Review,* Vol. 29 (1964), pp. 568–75;
E. L. McDill and J. S. Coleman, "Family and Peer Influences in College
Plans of High School Students," *Sociology of Education,* Vol. 38 (1965), pp.
112–26; E. Q. Campbell and C. N. Alexander, Jr., "Structural Effects and
Interpersonal Relationships," *American Journal of Sociology,* Vol. 71 (1965–
66), pp. 284–89.
47. McDill and Coleman, "Family and Peer Influences in College Plans of High
School Students."

member of the leading crowd is as strongly associated with their intention to attend college as is their family background. The effect of membership in the leading crowd is strongest in those high schools where college is a highly valued aspiration.

The effects of group status on college orientation can be explained as follows.[48] First, high-status cliques are apt to have a majority of members who plan to attend college. They are more often students from well-educated families, and because of the orientation of their families toward college, most students in the leading crowd are apt to be college-oriented. Students in these cliques who initially did not plan to attend college are influenced by the values of the group to shift to a college orientation, so that by the senior year a larger proportion of these high-status students are college-oriented.

Conversely, those with a noncollege orientation who do not belong to the high-status cliques are more apt to associate with others having similar attitudes and to be further influenced to reject college. The influence of peer-group selection may extend to selection of courses, which itself is related to likelihood of college attendance.

This same study also indicates that the college orientation of the leading crowd is due not to interest in academic studies, but rather to the attraction of campus social life, freedom from parental control, college athletics, and similar features of college life. High school students admire the boy who is a star athlete and the girl who is popular. Being a brilliant student is less valued and is associated with conformity, good grades, and gold stars dispensed by teachers. In the high-status cliques there is a net movement away from scholastic achievement from the freshman to the senior year, despite the increased plans for going to college. For those exceptional students outside the leading crowd who want college, this desire is more often associated with a positive orientation toward *scholastic* achievement.[49]

OCCUPATIONAL AND GRADUATE SCHOOL ASPIRATIONS

We now consider the direction taken by the freshman who has entered college. One researcher asked over 33,000 June college graduates questions about their future career choices, and also about choices that they had made earlier in college. These data tell much

48. *Ibid.*
49. *Ibid.*

about the magnitude and types of change that take place in college and give some indication of influences that brought about these effects.[50]

Upon entering college, students are already fairly well along in their career choices.[51] The great majority know in general the kind of subject matter in which they are interested and the type of vocation for which they plan to prepare. What changes do take place are not extreme reorientations, but shifts to related fields. Even in the freshman year, there are strong relations between choice of field and such demographic characteristics as sex, social class, and academic performance; many of these relations still prevail in the senior year. This general conclusion concerning the definiteness of freshmen choices should probably be tempered by pointing out that such choices have been measured only retroactively, as recalled by the seniors in the sample. Such retroactive measures are apt to overemphasize consistency from the freshman to the senior year.[52]

Over the college years, education and business gain the greatest number of adherents and have the lowest loss rates. The remaining fields lose a substantial proportion of those originally planning to major in them. However, the social sciences, biological sciences, law, and the humanities attract more than enough students to replace those who transfer out. Engineering, medicine, the physical sciences, and other professions show net declines from the freshman to the senior year. Factors associated with selection of major fields may be summarized as follows.[53]

Choice of education as a field is associated with being female, not wanting to make a lot of money, wanting to work with people, being a Negro, being from a small home town, being from a low socioeconomic class, and being Protestant. As might be expected, business is more often chosen by men, by students wanting to make a lot of money. It is chosen by students lower in academic performance. Other characteristics were not strongly associated with this choice. Medicine is chosen as a career more often by men than

50. J. A. Davis, "Intellectual Climates in 135 American Colleges and Universities: A Study in 'Social Psychophysics,'" *Sociology of Education*, Vol. 37 (1963), pp. 110–28; *Great Aspirations* (Chicago: Aldine, 1964); *Undergraduate Career Decisions* (Chicago: Aldine, 1965).
51. *Ibid.*
52. *Ibid.*
53. *Ibid.*

by women. Among the men, wanting to work with people is a factor in choosing medicine. In general, high socioeconomic status and high academic performance is also associated with choice of medicine.[54]

Findings such as these indicate clearly that career choice has certain definite associations with various demographic and personal characteristics. In particular, this study emphasizes the point that, by the time they enter college, students are well along certain paths to occupational careers. These paths may have minor branches leading to closely related occupational fields, but they are apt to lack connections to paths leading off in grossly different directions.

Entering freshmen are rapidly socialized by older students and faculty.[55] Those freshmen who, upon entrance, place a high value upon getting good grades, in a few months modify this attitude downward toward a position more like that of their older classmates. In part, however, this may represent a shift toward revision of unrealistic expectations concerning grades and toward a more realistic level of aspiration.[56]

Other adaptations to the academic aspects of college life are rapidly made. Freshmen learn from upperclassmen which courses are easy or tough and become familiar with the idiosyncrasies of specific instructors, choosing to enroll with those who have compatible modes of managing a course. We should not, of course, identify grades wholly with intellectual achievement; it is possible for a student to acquire certain skills and knowledge not accurately reflected in grades.[57] But in view of the fact that grades are used widely by the faculty in evaluating students and by graduate schools as criteria for admission, a student's orientation toward grade-getting has important consequences for his future career.

The proportion of freshmen who aspire toward graduate school increases during the freshman year. This seems to result from contacts with upperclassmen who themselves are oriented toward graduate school.[58] At the same time, they become less concerned about getting good grades. The student's small circle of close friends ap-

54. *Ibid.*
55. W. L. Wallace, *Student Culture* (Chicago: Aldine, 1966).
56. L. A. Pervin, "Reality and Nonreality in Student Expectations of College," *Journal of Psychology*, Vol. 64 (1966), pp. 41–48.
57. Wallace, *op. cit.*
58. *Ibid.*

peared to share more closely with him his orientation toward graduate school than did his full circle of acquaintances. With respect to getting high grades, however, close friends were less likely than acquaintances to have similar attitudes.

Evidence has been found that aspirations toward graduate school rise most among freshmen who had low academic rank in high school and who are from lower socioeconomic levels. The data indicate that this rather surprising change occurs because graduate school aspirations are not based upon expectations of success, but rather upon the desire to be socially accepted by upperclassmen. To achieve social acceptance, these freshmen adopt the attitudes of upperclassmen toward graduate school.[59]

As noted in Chapter Three, school climate also affects graduate school aspirations. Colleges with an academic or intellectual climate send a much greater proportion of their students to graduate school. Such climates prevail at small, private, high-quality institutions more than at large, less selective, public institutions.[60] Although such schools may attract more than their share of talented freshmen who already have graduate school aspirations, both the student climate and faculty behavior intensify these aspirations.

Implications for the Classroom

The recognition that many children start school with inadequate preschool experiences has obvious implications. These children need special training and enrichment experiences to enable them to handle first-grade materials. One prime example of an attempt to meet this need is the Head Start program sponsored by the Office of Economic Opportunity. These programs are offered at the preschool level and are intended to provide children who have inadequate backgrounds with the experiences necessary to prepare them for regular schooling.

In spite of such programs, many children will enter the first grade inadequately prepared. Current thinking requires that the teacher identify the areas in which these children are weak and, insofar as possible, remedy them through proper instruction. Programs such as Head Start should be extended

---

59. *Ibid.*
60. Davis, "Intellectual Climates in 135 American Colleges and Universities: A Study in 'Social Psychophysics.'"

into school-age levels, so that disadvantaged children who fall behind can be promptly brought back up to par. This contrasts with the older attitude of regarding disadvantaged children as less intelligent and assuming that it is hopeless to expect them to perform as well as children from more favorable backgrounds.

More research is needed on methods and techniques of remedial education for children who lag behind the norm. It is quite possible that this problem will be largely solved through technological developments, such as computerized instruction that is tailored to the ability level of each individual pupil.

Low ability and poor skills, however, are not the only factors in poor classroom performance. Poor motivation produces poor performance and school dropouts. This lack of motivation appears to stem from family background and from the social factors that reinforce it, such as being surrounded by peers who likewise have low motivation and by encountering unfavorable teacher attitudes toward the poor performer. The family situation that provides little encouragement for the child's educational and occupational success can best be remedied by widespread social legislation that provides for a more equitable distribution of income and educational opportunity. Aside from this ultimate solution, the school and the classroom teacher can take active steps to involve parents from disadvantaged families in the problems of the school and in the education of their children.

Quite clearly, under most conditions ability grouping in the schools widens the gap between the high and low performer, as does the existence of schools having a predominance of children from a poor family background. This effect of grouping is explained by the support from one's peers for poor academic performance and by the positive emphasis that peers place on activities that interfere with good performance. Ability grouping enhances this effect in the lower groups and is thus disadvantageous to them. The abolition of segregation and a vigorous upgrading of schools in impoverished areas is required to improve the education of such children.

At more advanced educational levels, particularly in the case of racial minorities, the problem lies with society itself—there are too few appropriate job opportunities for the Negro with a college education. Similar prejudice exists for some other minority groups. If social action eventually brings about more equal opportunities, students from such minority groups may be expected to develop a more serious interest in educational achievement.

Once again, research and the conclusions drawn from it here may be summarized largely in a single vital principle: success experiences are essential in creating the motivation to perform well in school and in acquiring the basic skills that are prerequisite to later performances. Many disadvantaged children start school with a sense of inadequacy. This feeling and their lack of preschool preparation insures that they will have too few success and too many failure experiences. These experiences are the second stage in a cycle that leads ever downward, and there is little in the present structure of school systems that is designed to break this cycle of defeat and despair.

Chapter Five

Effects of
Classroom Interaction

So far we have discussed the effects of the family and of the school environment on the performance of the student; we have deferred until this point a discussion of what is probably the most significant aspect of the school situation: interaction in the classroom. At the elementary and high school level, at least, it is in the classroom that friendships are formed and intimate peer groups emerge; among the various school representatives, it is the classroom teacher with whom the pupil has the most interaction. As a basis for this discussion, we will review a number of social psychological concepts and principles.

The behavior of teacher and student in the classroom reveals certain regularities of feeling, thought, and action. In part, these regularities arise out of shared expectations that group members have with respect to each other's behavior. When a teacher calls a class to order, he expects certain modifications in behavior, and the students in turn know what these are. These expectations, or norms, channel much of human interaction and are the basic elements of the *institutional structure*. A number of terms conceptualize these patterned interactions, as follows.

The expectations that group members share for each other's behavior are called *role expectations*. *Role* refers to the expectation that group members have for those individuals (or *actors*) who fall in a particular category of persons or who occupy a given position in the group. In the school, a number of categories of actors may be distinguished, such as teacher, pupil, principal, or school nurse. The behavior relevant to these expectations is referred to as *role behavior*.

A person is expected to behave in a way that conforms to his role category. If he does not, members of the group exert pressures on him to conform. In the school situation, these actions (called sanctions) may vary from the simple expression of approval or disapproval, through group ostracizing, to more formal procedures such as suspension of a student or dismissal of a teacher. These systems of expectations and related sanctions constitute the *structure* of various institutions. Thus, we speak of the educational institution, the institution of the family, and so on.

A second source of stability in the behavior of persons lies in the *subinstitutional structure*. This consists of regularities of thought, feeling, and action that arise out of and are continuously maintained by the direct exchange of primary rewards between parties in interaction. Whereas *institutional* regularities persist because persons are constrained to conform to role expectations by the application of sanctions involving such secondary reinforcers as money or social approval, *subinstitutional* regularities persist because of rewards *intrinsic* to the interaction. Thus, friendship emerges and is maintained between two persons because each is directly gratified by the behavior of the other. In contrast, a marriage relationship might be maintained even though both parties found the behavior of the partner unrewarding, unpleasant, or frustrating, simply because they, as well as others, shared the expectation that marriage should not end in divorce. Most marriages and other relationships have both institutional and subinstitutional sources of support, if for no other reason than that very soon, even in a relatively noninstitutionalized relation such as friendship, norms emerge which govern much of the interaction. But even though most relations involve both institutional and subinstitutional controls, the distinction is a useful one, particularly in the analyses of such relatively institutionalized task groups as the factory or school.

Institutional structures are organized around the achievement of important social values or ends. The family's function is to socialize the child. The function of the political institution is to maintain order. In contrast, subinstitutional structures are delineated in terms of *individual* dimensions of feeling, thought, and action. Hence we speak of the *affect structure* or *sociometric structure*, consisting of the feelings of attraction and repulsion between members of a group, or the *power structure*, delineating the pattern of subordination and superordination among group members. For the most part, this chapter will treat the lesser-known and lesser-understood subinstitutional aspects of classroom interaction, although we will also touch occasionally on those aspects of the institutional structure that affect the workings of subinstitutional structures in the school situation.

THE SUBINSTITUTIONAL STRUCTURE

This section deals briefly with the determinants of various subinstitutional structures; the next section will discuss their impact on student behavior.

The term *sociometric structure* has traditionally been used to describe the patterns of positive and negative affect, attraction and repulsion, that exist between members of a group. Typically this has been explored through the administration of a sociometric test which asks group members to indicate their choices of others, on the basis of some criterion. In a classroom the pupils may be asked to choose each other as seat mates, as partners in some joint project, and so on. The resulting choices can be analyzed in a number of ways,[1] although the most widely known method is that of constructing a sociogram. This consists of a spatial arrangement of persons, designated by points or small circles on a plane, with arrows indicating the direction of choice. The intensity of attraction or repulsion is reflected in the distance between persons. As the sample sociogram shows, persons connected by two solid lines, indicating mutual choice, are closer than two persons connected by a single solid line, a nonreciprocated choice. The latter pair are closer than two people neither of whom chooses each other, and these in turn are closer than two persons one or both of whom reject each other as associates. While this method of presentation is less precise than other methods and becomes increasingly difficult to use as the size of the group increases, it does allow rather easy designation of such structural features as small subgroups or cliques (see persons 1, 2, 3, 4, and 5); persons with high choice status, or sociometric *stars* (see person 5); persons who are targets of considerable hostility (see person 8); and, finally, those who are almost isolates in the group (see person 10).

The choice pattern differs somewhat with the choice criterion employed. A child frequently chosen as a seat mate may be chosen

---

1. C. H. Proctor and C. P. Loomis, "Analysis of Sociometric Data," in M. Jahoda, M. Deutsch, and S. W. Cook, eds., *Research Methods in Social Relations* (New York: Holt, Rinehart and Winston, 1951), Vol. 2, pp. 561–85.

A SAMPLE SOCIOGRAM

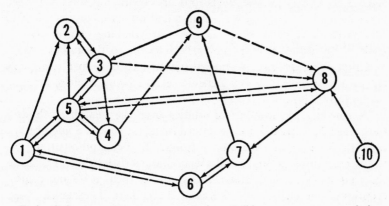

Each circle represents a group member. Solid arrows represent choices; broken arrows, rejection. (Adapted from *Research Methods in Social Relations*, Vol. 2, by Marie Jahoda, Morton Deutsch, and Stuart W. Cook. Copyright 1951 by Holt, Rinehart and Winston, Inc. Reproduced by permission of Holt, Rinehart and Winston, Inc.)

less frequently as a work partner or as the chooser's teammate in a game. Two general types of criteria of choice have been distinguished. *Psychegroup* criteria involve choices based on a person's ability to satisfy the chooser's socioemotional needs. Persons chosen by a general criterion such as "friend" or by a more specific one such as "spend one's leisure time with" are instances of choices based on psychegroup criteria. Whereas a choice on the basis of psychegroup criteria represents a desire to associate with another as an end in itself, choice on the basis of *sociogroup* criteria is a means to some other end such as goal achievement. A person chosen on the criterion of "work with" may well reflect the chooser's desire to work with whoever is best able to contribute to the job to be done. Among children a teammate may well be chosen for his skill rather than for his personal congeniality. This distinction is useful because the resultant sociometric structure is apt to differ depending on which type of criterion is used.

In general, the structure of a psychegroup involves a wider dispersion of choice and a higher degree of mutuality than the structure of a sociogroup because in the former the choices reflect to some degree the uniqueness of the socioemotional needs of each member. For example, members who like to gossip are mutually attracted, dependent persons are attracted to nurturant ones, and those who like serious conversations are drawn together. The concentration of choices in a sociogram based on a sociogroup criterion reflects the fact that group members are making choices on the basis of the same criteria, the skills relevant to the task at hand, and that these are usually not distributed equally in a group. In such a group one or a few persons receive many choices, and the others only a few.

A considerable number of studies over the last three decades have been concerned with the determinants of choice. Some of these have been made in classroom settings.[2] Earlier studies attempted to discover those personal and social characteristics that distinguish the frequently chosen person. Later studies focused on the characteristics of the chooser as well as of the chosen. The age-old question of whether opposite or similar persons are attracted to each other was a persistent theme of these later studies. The main findings of these studies may be summarized as follows:

A person is likely to choose the following individuals: (1) those with whom he has a greater opportunity to interact, (2) those who have characteristics most desirable in terms of the norms and values of the group, (3) those who are most similar to him in attitudes, values, and social-background characteristics, (4) those whom he perceives as choosing him or assigning favorable characteristics to him, (5) those who see him as he sees himself, and (6) those in whose company he has experienced need satisfaction.

Exchange theory, as discussed in Chapter Three, appears to account adequately for these findings. A person is attracted to another individual to the extent that the reward-cost outcomes of interaction with the other exceed his comparison level. Accordingly, popular persons would be those whose behavior has wide reward value. Unpopular ones would be those whose behavior is seldom rewarding and often costly. In a college-dormitory study, the most popular residents were regarded as considerate, sincere, and objective in their interest in others, as helping others, giving compliments, offering encouragement, and so on. In contrast, those least popular were egocentric, attention-demanding, and dominating.[3]

---

2. N. E. Gronlund, *Sociometry in the Classroom* (New York: Harper & Row, 1959).
3. M. E. Bonney, R. E. Hoblet, and A. H. Dreyer, "A Study of Some Factors Related to Sociometric Status in a Men's Dormitory," *Sociometry*, Vol. 16 (1953), pp. 287–301.

A similar picture emerged in a study of the rejected college male.[4] The same kinds of differences were also found between popular and unpopular girls in a training school [5] and among public school children.[6]

Bonds of attraction emerge between those persons in a group who can meet each other's needs at low cost. The need for consensual validation, that is, the need of a person to find in others support for his attitudes and values (particularly his attitude toward himself) appears to be an important need satisfied by friendship. A study of the development of friendship patterns in a college living group reported increasing similarity over time in values and in attitudes toward various issues and other group members between those who chose each other on successive administrations of a sociometric instrument.[7] Factors making it possible to explore the need-satisfying potentialities of another person at low cost similarly foster attraction, because the rewards minus the costs are likely to be high. Hence, in a school situation one would expect pupils who are physically closer to choose each other more often. The point about comparison levels should also be kept in mind. Two children whose behavior and other characteristics are not highly valued by other children in the group may find satisfaction in a mutual friendship because the lack of rewards from others and the lack of alternative friendships has reduced the comparison level of both.

If a teacher were to determine the sociometric structure by asking students to choose the persons whom they felt were best qualified to represent their class at a student conference, the resultant structure of choice would probably be more descriptive of the *status* structure than of the *affect* or *friendship* structure. The status structure consists of rankings of group members on a variety of dimensions or characteristics deemed important to the group. In American society, wealth, occupational prestige, educational attainment, and ethnic or racial origin are status dimensions. Among high

---

4. J. W. Kidd, "An Analysis of Social Rejection in a College Men's Residence Hall," *Sociometry*, Vol. 14 (1951), pp. 226–34.

5. H. H. Jennings, *Leadership and Isolation*, 2nd ed. (London: Longmans, Green, 1950).

6. M. E. Bonney and P. J. Powell, "Differences in Social Behavior Between Sociometrically High and Sociometrically Low Children," *Journal of Educational Research*, Vol. 46 (1953), pp. 481–95.

7. T. M. Newcomb, *The Acquaintance Process* (New York: Holt, Rinehart and Winston, 1961).

school students, status dimensions include family background, athletic prowess, and academic proficiency.[8]

In groups of children, as well as of adults, persons vary in the degree to which they can influence each other's behavior. While early investigations were guided by the idea that power is a personal attribute, most contemporary theories implicitly or explicitly recognize that the power of one person over another depends not only on the resources of the former but also on the dependencies or needs of the latter and the alternatives open to him for need satisfaction. One child may have considerable power over others in the group who wish to organize a ball game if he owns the only baseball. However, should the group interests shift to some other activity or should their alternatives improve as a result of the willingness of someone else to contribute a ball, his power, based on this resource at least, is eliminated. Important resources are those which are relevant to powerful human needs. The ability to satisfy others' needs for affection and status, for instance, is an important resource.

Various investigations suggest that this is an important resource underlying power in children's groups.[9] For example, in a group of boys aged twelve to fourteen, the following characteristics, in the order given, were associated with high power: helpfulness, fairness, sociability, expertness, fearlessness, and physical strength. We can distinguish a number of types of power dependent on particular underlying resources.[10] *Reward* power is based on the ability to *reward* another, *coercive* power on the ability to punish. *Expert* power rests in the possession of knowledge that another wishes to use to satisfy his needs. *Referent* power is based on the desire of others to be like or to identify with the powerful person. Finally, *legitimate* power rests on the shared expectation that one person should accept influence and direction from another.

The power that a teacher has over his pupils often contains elements of all five types of power. By virtue of his age and size, as well as his access to various institutionalized sanctions such as grades or the right to send a pupil to the principal's office for

---

8. J. S. Coleman, *The Adolescent Society* (New York: Macmillan, 1961).

9. M. Gold, "Power in the Classroom," *Sociometry*, Vol. 21 (1958), pp. 50–60; S. Rosen, G. Levinger, and R. Lippitt, "Perceived Sources of Social Power," *Journal of Abnormal Social Psychology*, Vol. 62 (1961), pp. 439–41.

10. J. R. P. French, Jr., and B. H. Raven, "The Bases of Social Power," in Dorwin Cartwright, ed., *Studies in Social Power* (Ann Arbor: University of Michigan Press, 1959), pp. 118–44.

disciplinary action, he can both reward and punish the child. His superior knowledge relative to that of his pupils makes it likely that they will follow his lead. His power, augmented both by his status and, where he is liked, by the positive regard of the student, also may facilitate identification, the process underlying referent power. Finally, he exercises legitimate power by virtue of his role as teacher. He, like his pupils, has learned to expect that he will be the leader in classroom activities.

We will discuss leadership in a later section; however, let us briefly distinguish here *leadership* and *power*. Although a leader exercises power, persons with high power are not necessarily leaders. Two elements are relevant to this distinction. First, *leadership* is the exercise of power that moves the group toward its task and maintenance goals. A *leader* helps direct the group toward accomplishing environmentally imposed goals and sees that the internal relations of the group are such as to insure enough satisfaction of the socioemotional needs of its members to motivate them to remain in the group and work toward its goals. Second, the power of a recognized leader is legitimate power. He exerts influence as a leader because he and others believe it to be his right and obligation to do so. This is obvious in the case of the teacher in the classroom. That an informal leader, such as a fellow pupil, has legitimate power is less obvious, yet this element is present. In a situation demanding leadership other classmates expect this pupil to exercise influence.

If one were to observe over time the frequency and direction of communicative acts (verbal exchanges, significant nods and glances, and the passing of notes), certain patterns would emerge. In most classrooms the teacher is involved more frequently than other group members in communication exchanges. This is in large part a product of the institutionalized structure, the system of expectations, which dictates that the teacher initiate most of the communication. The participation of each of the other group members is also somewhat distinct. Pupils, whether they be first graders or members of a graduate seminar, vary in the frequency and direction of their communicative acts. These characteristic differences have been demonstrated to be a product of both individual and group factors.[11]

---

11. E. F. Borgatta and R. F. Bales, "Interaction of Individuals in Reconstituted Groups," *Sociometry*, Vol. 16 (1953), pp. 302–20.

Individuals, as a function of their unique personality needs, vary in their characteristic rates of communication. These rates, however, are never simply a function of individual characteristics. The rate of communication of an individual varies from group to group. In part this is a function of the rates of communication of other persons in the group as these are influenced by their respective personality dynamics; in part, however, this reflects the person's position in the structures of affect, power, and status in these groups. In one group, because of his position in these structures, a person is both allowed and encouraged by the reactions of others to communicate actively. In another, where his position differs, he may communicate only infrequently. The child who is almost mute in class and a chatterbox at home or on the playground is a concrete example.

The direction of communication in a group is similarly subject to a variety of constraints. In non-task groups, or in task groups where the demands of the situation are temporarily relaxed, communication tends to flow along the lines of the affect or friendship structure.[12] In fact, under these circumstances a record of those who talk with each other is often a good indicator of the patterns of attraction in the group.

The status and power structures also affect the flow of communication, in that two conflicting communication tendencies stem from them. First is the tendency for a person to direct his communications upward in the status and power hierarchies. This has been demonstrated in two experiments [13] and in an analysis of communication patterns among adult participants at a conference.[14] In the former, more communication was directed toward group members who were working on a task designated as more important; in the latter, psychiatrists, who have more status and power, re-

---

12. Josephine Klein, *The Study of Groups* (London: Routledge & Kegan Paul, 1956); L. Festinger, D. Cartwright, K. Barber, J. Fleischl, J. Gottsdanker, A. Keysen, and G. Leavitt, "A Study of Rumor: Its Origin and Spread," *Human Relations,* Vol. 1 (1948), pp. 464–86.

13. H. H. Kelley, "Communication in Experimentally Created Hierarchies," *Human Relations,* Vol. 4 (1951), pp. 39–56; A. R. Cohen, "Upward Communication in Experimentally Created Hierarchies," *Human Relations,* Vol. 11 (1958), pp. 41–53.

14. J. I. Hurwitz, A. Zander and B. Hymovitch, "Some Effects of Power on the Relations Among Group Members," in D. Cartwright and A. Zander, eds., *Group Dynamics: Research and Theory,* 2nd ed. (New York: Harper & Row, 1960).

ceived more communications than clinical psychologists and social workers. A second tendency is to communicate with persons who are equal in status. A study of ninth- and tenth-grade girls has shown that they most often received communications from other girls having a status equal to their own.[15]

An analysis of the rewards and costs persons experience when they communicate explains these effects of the subinstitutional structures on communication patterns. When friends communicate, they exchange rewards. One of the most common forms of exchange between friends is *consensual validation*. This takes the form of a repeated confirmation of each other's value statements. Friends express agreement on persons and activities that they like or dislike.

It has been suggested that, under favorable circumstances, when an individual communicates to a person of higher status he shares that status vicariously and also enjoys an increase in status because persons attribute similar status to those who associate with one another. Under other circumstances, however, communication upward is accompanied by the costs of anxiety over possible rejection, with a consequent loss of status, as well as the receipt of less rewarding responses from those of higher status. Since those high in status prefer interaction with others as high or higher than themselves, they will be less motivated to continue a relation by providing high rewards to their low-status partners. Consequently interaction with one's equals may be preferred because it is both safe and provides maximum outcomes.

As previously noted, much interaction is normatively structured by the roles of teacher and pupil. For the most part the content of these roles reflects the formal goals of the educational institution. Roles are structured to facilitate the acquisition of knowledge and skills, the physical and social development of the student, and similar educational goals. These constitute but part of the normative structure influencing behavior. Other informal expectations arise; some of these may facilitate the achievement of educational goals, some may be irrelevant to them, and still others may interfere with educational goals.

These informal expectations emerge under one of two circumstances: (1) where the formal system of expectations fails to achieve

---

15. M. Riley *et al.*, "Interpersonal Orientations in Small Groups: A Consideration of the Questionnaire Approach," *American Sociological Review*, Vol. 19 (1954), pp. 715–24.

task goals or (2) in response to needs of group members that are unrelated to task goals. The latter is a particularly important source of informal expectations, because when persons interact they normally seek to satisfy a variety of needs in addition to task-related ones. In the classroom, students are motivated not only to learn but also to satisfy such socioemotional needs as being liked, being admired by others, or having others confirm one's attitudes and values concerning oneself and the world.

Two pervasive norms related to socioemotional needs are of particular significance in understanding work-group performances, because frequently their effect is at variance with those of the structure of formal or official norms. Typically arising in work groups, the first of these informal norms defines an *adequate level of performance*. This is often called a *restrictive norm* because it typically defines an adequate level of performance which is below that specified as desirable by the institutional structure. In the classroom, for instance, teachers may expect that all students will strive at least for above average grades, B's and A's. Incentive systems of payment in factories similarly assume that workers will strive to maximize their production and earnings. There is evidence from both industrial [16] and educational [17] settings that informal norms specify a lower output. While a number of explanations have been offered for this, one persuasive argument suggests that these norms function to limit the destructive costs of competition, particularly as these affect the need to maintain a favorable self image. Informal norms generally prescribe a level of production that most can achieve; in the classroom it is the "gentleman's C." Frequently, however, these normative influences are less definite and explicit, simply taking the form of disapproval of those who over-exert themselves. Such disapproval is implicit in the derogatory flavor of names applied to the overachiever: eager beaver, slave, rate buster, greasy grind, and so on.

A second rather pervasive norm in work groups, and one which again functions to reduce competition, is that which prescribes social distance between the formal leader and his followers, between the

16. F. J. Roethlisberger and W. J. Dickson, *Management and the Worker* (Cambridge: Harvard University Press, 1939).
17. Coleman, *op. cit.;* E. Hughes, H. Becker, and B. Geer, "Student Culture and Academic Effort," in N. Sanford, ed., *The American College* (New York: Wiley, 1962).

foreman and his workers, the teacher and his pupils. The norm against apple polishing or any of its more vivid but less polite epithets restricts the unfair use of personal relations to gain favors from the leader. Informal norms are important in the explanation of productivity and satisfaction in the classroom as well as in problems of discipline. We say more about these norms in the following section.

ONGOING PROCESSES IN THE CLASSROOM

This section applies the previously described concepts to an understanding of the ongoing process of interaction in the classroom. In a typical school, some activities are related to its formal goals, as when children are reading or listening to the recitations of a classmate or to the teacher. Other activities are obviously irrelevant, such as the horseplay when a group ostensibly collaborating on a project has momentarily abandoned its work. The proportion of task-related and task-irrelevant behavior varies from group to group. When teachers comment that one class is better than another they often mean that one group is very hardworking, diligent, and industrious and another is much less so. The ratio of task to non-task activities varies also within a given class from one time to another. There are periods when classroom members are more engrossed in task activities and periods when they are less productive. In fact, as in all work groups, there is a certain rhythm to task activity, with bursts of non-task activity following periods of intensive work.

Close observation is not necessary to discern in any class variations among individuals in the ratio of task to non-task behaviors; some are more diligent scholars than others. While these variations are in part affected by personal abilities, skills, and temperament, they are not independent of group processes. The balance of task and non-task activity, as well as variations in this balance from person to person, is a function of the outcomes that group members experience relative to both kinds of activities. The rewards and costs experienced from either stem from three major sources. First, the activity itself may be more or less intrinsically rewarding or costly. Some activities, such as those involved in play, are more rewarding and less costly than others, such as memorizing a series of algebraic operations. Second, an activity may be associated with the rewards of achieving an important goal, which may be either related to the task or independent of it. For most individuals, the desire to be popular is an important goal. Finally, a third source of favorable or unfavorable outcomes associated with task or non-task activities consists of a variety of *reactions* from oneself and others that are consequences of conformity to normative expectations. In some groups, such as athletic teams, members are rewarded to the degree that they conform to the expectation that they should exert every effort toward achievement of the task goals. In other groups, persons are punished in a variety of ways for working too hard. We have already noted in some detail the origin and nature of restrictive norms in task groups.

The relative importance of these rewards and costs will vary for different individuals and for the same individual at different points in time depending on both his needs, abilities, and skills and his alternatives for rewarding experience in other social contexts. A number of studies in educational settings support this proposition. Conformity to peer-group norms was shown to be greater for those students who were most dependent on the group.[18] Similarly, differences in scholastic achievement may in part reflect differences in the motivational value of positive evaluation by teachers for various individuals.[19] To the degree that a person has internalized the norms of the group, he experiences such self-administered rewards and costs as pride and guilt in response to his conformity to or deviation from the norms.

To illustrate the relation of these variables to the balance and distribution of task and non-task behavior in a class, it might be useful to state how conditions should combine to maximize task behavior at the expense of non-task behavior.

In such an instance the task activity would involve high intrinsic rewards at minimum cost for all members of the group. Competing non-task behavior must have low psychic value. The absorption of a group of young children in the early phases of a story-telling session or of a group of medical students observing a famous surgeon performing a difficult operation would be examples. The goals of the

---

18. W. J. McKeachie *et al.*, "Student Affiliation Motive, Teacher Warmth, and Academic Achievement," *Journal of Personality and Social Psychology*, Vol. 4, No. 4 (1966), pp. 457–61; W. L. Wallace, *Student Culture* (Chicago: Aldine, 1966).
19. J. McDavid, Jr., "Some Relationships Between Social Reinforcement and Scholastic Achievement," *Journal of Consulting Psychology*, Vol. 23 (1959), pp. 151–54.

task activity must overshadow non-task goals to a maximum degree. They should be related in direct and immediate fashion to powerful and salient needs. The burst of task activity that is often noted in a group as its members become aware that a prized goal is almost within reach and can be attained by a final, all-out effort illustrates this condition. A further requirement is that the normative expectations of the group favor task activity at the expense of other behavior; the affect, status, power, and leadership structures of the group must also be consistent with maximizing conformity to norms of task excellence, as well as with organizing and channeling the resources of all members of the group toward successful task performance.

An examination of the sources of departures from this ideal case may clarify the origin of many difficulties the teacher faces in his attempt to achieve this almost impossible maximum of task behavior. More than leaders of other types of groups, educators have been aware that task activity must be made intrinsically satisfying. Many curriculum innovations in the past quarter of a century were aimed at increasing the rewards and decreasing the costs of school work. The general trend away from memorization and toward creative problem-solving illustrates this. Yet, certain information must be retained, and certain skills developed. This objective requires tedious practice and thus increases the cost of learning.

Education theorists have long been convinced of the necessity for showing the relevance of classwork to goals important to the child. Bringing the world into the classroom to show the child the relevance of what he is learning is in part a response to this philosophy. Nevertheless, many learning tasks cannot be related even vicariously to important goals of the child. At best such tasks may be portrayed as important to him because of their relation to goals he will have as an adult. He is told that he must learn arithmetic so that he can later learn the higher mathematics necessary to become an engineer. Even the goal of a good report card, a desirable one for most children, is often too distant from the actual learning activity to be effective.

Teachers have been less aware of a third source of rewards and costs in the classroom, those associated with conformity to group norms. It is in this area that insights from a social psychological analysis of classroom interaction can be of the greatest value. Rewards and costs experienced in response to the behavior of others in the learning situation are particularly potent forces for two reasons. First, they involve giving or withdrawing affection and respect, rewards and punishments that are related to powerful drives. Second, unlike the previously described set of rewards, they are likely to follow immediately a particular act and, hence, are maximally effective. Whether these rewards and punishments favor task or non-task activities depends on the character of the norms. Ideally the norms prescribe maximum effort in the *task* area. As we have previously noted, however, this is generally not the case in work groups. Norms arise in many situations that set a standard of performance below that level considered optimum from the standpoint of the formal goals of the organization. It has been suggested that a major function of the norms is to protect persons from excessive competition by encouraging a level of productivity that most if not all can achieve. One would expect that such norms would develop and find maximum adherence where the costs of competition are highly salient. A major cost in competitive activity is anxiety over the possibility of invidious comparison, of being evaluated as less worthy as a person because of one's poor showing relative to others in some activity.

Two principles suggest that the school setting maximizes both the motivation and the opportunity to make such comparisons, even when they are likely to be costly to some group members.[20] First, persons make comparisons under conditions where the behavior in question and its evaluation are readily observable. Students recite, present papers, and work on problems at the blackboard before their peers. Similarly, grading systems in most schools provide summary indicators in the form of letter grades, percentiles, honors, and so on that facilitate interpersonal comparisons by teachers, parents, and pupils.

Second, persons are likely to compare themselves with others whom they consider similar to themselves. The classroom facilitates the perception of similarity. Age-graded classes eliminate the possibility of differentiating oneself from others according to age. Differences in inherent intellectual capacities are also minimized. Unlike differences in size and weight, there is nothing about a person's appearance that might enable one to discern such differences. Real

20. Leon Festinger, "A Theory of Social Comparison Processes," *Human Relations,* Vol. 7 (1954), pp. 117–40; J. W. Thibaut and H. H. Kelley, *The Social Psychology of Groups* (New York: Wiley, 1959).

differences are in fact likely to be reduced by the practice of ability grouping. Further, the pervasive democratic ideology in our culture, along with concern for the mental health of the child, has generally worked against making these differences visible.

For these reasons the child is apt to compare his performance in the classroom with all comers. This is not so on the playground or athletic field. Here cues to differences in performance are obvious, and children are less prone to compare themselves with those of visibly superior endowment. This is one reason why restrictive norms are much less in evidence in this sphere of school activity.

The contrast between success on the athletic field and in the classroom contains another element that should be considered—the structure of the task. Some tasks, by the manner in which they are organized, engender powerful interpersonal pressures toward excellence. Team athletics, where success for all members hinges on each doing his part well, creates strong normative pressures in favor of all-out efforts to win.[21] Most classroom activities, in contrast, are not organized as group projects, and a potentially powerful source of task motivation is relatively untapped.

The obviousness of the costs of invidious comparison should not lead us to overlook other costs that may arise in a situation fostering restrictive norms. Where the activity itself is more costly than rewarding, as is much school work, competitive pressure that might otherwise encourage productivity at uncomfortable levels is kept in check by these norms. Further, these normative influences need not take the form of explicit rules prescribing a given level of performance. On occasion they might be explicit, as shown in a study of medical students where informal norms emerged specifying which and how many case summations out of the total assigned would actually be turned in.[22] More often, however, these normative influences are reflected in a certain degree of dislike for those who spend too much time and energy in task activity.

Another set of normative influences operating in most work groups, including those in an educational setting, appears to arise when satisfying non-task activity is threatened. Failure to cooperate in such activities is apt to arouse the resentment of peers. The student who refuses to pass on a note in class or to collaborate in a classroom prank is open to various forms of derogation, ranging

---

21. Coleman, *op. cit.*
22. Hughes, Becker, and Geer, *op. cit.*

from name-calling to more serious punishment, perhaps even physical attack. Since most official school rules encourage task activity and discourage non-task activity, those who report violations of these rules are particularly the target of negative sanctions. So pervasive is this norm in social life that not even the teacher may particularly care for the tattletale. Such norms serve to protect non-task satisfactions.

At this point variations in the effectiveness of sanctions in different groups and from person to person within the same group may be discussed. A group can exert pressures on its members to conform to norms *to the degree* that they are *attracted* to the group.[23] A group to which members are strongly attracted is characterized as "cohesive." Highly cohesive groups are capable of exerting maximum conformity pressure. In terms of exchange theory, cohesion is a function of the degree to which group members' *outcomes* exceed their *comparison levels*. Outcomes are high to the extent that the group activities are intrinsically rewarding, lead to the achievement of highly valued goals, and produce high levels of satisfaction of the members' socioemotional needs. Comparison levels are low to the degree that satisfactions have been low in the past, and alternative sources of satisfaction are low. Where such conditions obtain, creating high cohesiveness, classroom group norms are likely to be maximally effective.

Since outcomes and comparison levels vary from person to person, each will be differentially receptive to such group pressures, particularly to the degree that he perceives that his position will be altered by his conformity. The person who is low in the affect or status structure and who perceives that conformity will improve his position is particularly receptive to conformity pressures. Another person similarly low, but who has no hope of changing his position, may be much less receptive to such pressures. A third person secure in his *high* status will similarly be less receptive. Empirical findings consistent with these conclusions have been observed in studies of experimental groups in laboratory settings,[24] as well as in ongoing

---

23. D. Cartwright and A. Zander, *op. cit.*
24. H. H. Kelley and M. M. Shapiro, "An Experiment in Conformity to Group Norms Where Conformity Is Detrimental to Group Achievement," *American Sociological Review*, Vol. 19 (1954), pp. 667–77; J. E. Dittes and H. H. Kelley, "Effects of Different Conditions of Acceptance on Conformity to Group Norms," *Journal of Abnormal Social Psychology*, Vol. 53 (1956), pp. 100–07.

work groups in natural settings.[25] They have been specifically demonstrated in school groups.[26]

The degree to which task compared to non-task activities are encouraged by the normative climate of the classroom is primarily influenced by the power structure. While norms protect and enhance the outcomes of group members, they do not contribute to the outcomes of all equally. Those members with greater power play a greater role in their formation. This fact of group life produces marked differences in the normative climate from classroom to classroom. At one extreme, classroom control breaks down completely when powerful student leaders are able to influence the group to interfere with task activities; or, at the other extreme, the powerful teacher is able to control classroom activity completely.

While the latter situation often suggests a teacher who rules through fear, this is not necessarily the case. The teacher who can exert a variety of noncoercive forms of power may have greater control, since these forms are more likely to alter the normative structure. The kindergarten teacher adored by his young charges or the charismatic teacher of a group of graduate students illustrates this.

In most classrooms, the balance of power is less extreme, with normative influences and other forms of power less exclusively supporting either task or non-task activity. For the sake of exposition, however, we might deal with two extremes: (1) where a teacher's power maximizes task behavior and (2) where his power is minimal. A teacher is likely to be most successful where he has resources on which his students are dependent, where their alternatives to compliance have low outcomes, and where task activity is associated with high rewards and low costs. We have previously distinguished between forms of power in terms of the resources of the power figure and the dependencies of the persons influenced. The use of each form has consequences for subsequent control: the exercise of various types of power may strengthen subsequent control, weaken it, or leave it unaffected.

Reward and coercive power are high where the teacher can markedly affect student satisfactions, as when students are highly

25. P. Blau, *The Dynamics of Bureaucracy* (Chicago: University of Chicago Press, 1955); A. Zaleznik, C. R. Christensen, and F. J. Roethlisberger, "The Motivation, Productivity and Satisfaction of Workers: A Prediction Study" (Harvard University Bureau of Business Research, 1958).

26. McKeachie *et al., op. cit.;* Wallace, *op. cit.*

motivated to get good grades. Where pupils are less motivated toward grades, the teacher's power stemming from this resource is reduced. The *continued* use of reward power has some consequences which decrease and some which augment the teacher's future power. On the one hand, continual application of the same rewards reduces their effectiveness because the needs they satisfy become satiated. The lavish use of praise, for instance, may be less effective than if it had been given more sparingly. But the use of rewards is apt to augment both the *referent* and the legitimate power of the teacher. There is evidence to suggest that persons identify with those who reward them.[27] To the degree that identification leads the child to adopt the teacher's norms, the legitimate power of the teacher over the child is also enhanced. These forms of power are particularly important since they create in the child the motivation to excel in task activities. One other condition also favors identification. Evidence indicates that the more one person perceives another as similar to himself (for example, in age, sex, race, and other characteristics), the more he is apt to identify with that other. Such identification augments the power of the latter over the former.

Finally, the evidence that student performance is associated with a teacher's competence in a given area suggests the operation of expert power. Many studies indicate that communications from experts are more accepted than communications from non-experts. In one study, the rate of student improvement in high school science classes was positively related to the teacher's having done his undergraduate work at some institution other than a teacher's college and having taken a relatively large number of science courses.[28] While student performance may in part be due to the teacher's greater knowledge of his subject matter, it may also be augmented by the greater influence he wields because of his expertness.

The power of the teacher is not the only factor affecting performance. To the degree that other high-power figures in the group are predisposed toward task activity, the general climate of the group will be favorable. Since peers are favored as models for

27. Albert Bandura, "Social Learning Through Imitation," *Nebraska Symposium on Motivation* (Lincoln: University of Nebraska Press, 1962), pp. 211–69; A. Bandura and A. C. Huston, "Identification as a Process of Incidental Learning," *Journal of Abnormal Social Psychology*, Vol. 63 (1961), pp. 311–18.
28. K. E. Anderson, "A Frontal Attack on the Basic Problem in Evaluation: The Achievement of the Objectives of Instruction in Specific Areas," *Journal of Experimental Education*, Vol. 18 (1950), pp. 163–74.

identification on the basis of their similarity as well as their media-
tion of important rewards, they are particularly potent sources of
influence. The ideal situation in the classroom is probably one
similar to that observed by Fiedler for a variety of work groups. The
leader in these work groups had close relations with his key man—
in the classroom this would be one or more powerful and popular
students—who served to set the direction toward enthusiastic task
participation.[29] However, where high-power pupils are in league
against the teacher, the norms that emerge among the students are
likely to favor task-disruptive and non-task activities.

Thus, the relationship between the teacher and those students
with high power is crucial. We have already noted that to the degree
that task activity and the goals involved are associated with
markedly more favorable outcomes than non-task activities, performance will be high. This is particularly important with respect
to the outcomes experienced by high-power members. Where the
particular task activity is incompatible with their skills and preferences, key students may well exert efforts favoring non-task
activity. Evidence suggests that where the status of high-power
members is threatened by poor performance in one area, they are
likely to encourage a shift into another area.[30] In a seventh-grade
class containing a number of boys who had been held back several
grades, these boys were undisputed peer-group leaders by virtue of
their size, strength, and athletic skills. In most of their classes, they
constantly disrupted task activities. Further evidence that teachers
who support the status structure of their classes have classrooms
with better social climates is consistent with this principle.[31]

Our discussion so far has emphasized those conditions favoring
task activities. Non-task behavior arises in response to unmet socioemotional needs. The level and salience of these needs depends on a
variety of factors in the classroom situation. We have previously
suggested that poor performance by a high-status person in a task
area may affect adversely the satisfaction of a variety of needs re-

29. F. E. Fiedler, "Interpersonal Perception and Group Effectiveness," in R.
Tagiuri and L. Petrullo, eds., *Person Perception and Interpersonal Behavior*
(Stanford: Stanford University Press, 1958), pp. 243–57.
30. J. F. Short, Jr., "Aggressive Behavior in Response to Status Threats," paper
read at American Sociological Association, New York, August 1960.
31. Lucy Polansky, "Group Social Climate and Teacher's Supportiveness of
Group Status Systems," *Journal of Educational Sociology*, Vol. 28 (1954), pp.
115–23.

lated to his status. This may not only prompt his withdrawal from the task area but also precipitate a variety of behaviors designed to increase his status, such as defying the teacher or clowning. While frustration of the socioemotional needs of a high-status member may be more disruptive because of his greater influence on others, it should be emphasized that similar frustration affecting any group member may lead to forms of behavior that interfere with task performances. Such a child may, although perhaps less successfully, become a showoff or a bully or may simply withdraw. While withdrawal from a classroom situation where his needs for status and affection go unmet does not interfere with the task behavior of other members, it reduces that student's involvement in the task area. Low sociometric choice status, particularly if perceived by the child, may cause poorer utilization of abilities by lowering his attraction to the school situation, and also by negatively affecting his self concept.[32] We should note that high choice status is not necessarily associated with good performance and low status with the reverse. The relation will depend on the child's perception of his status, the norm of his group, the degree to which the child's personality needs make him dependent on the group, and the availability of alternatives.

Other needs, beyond those for status and affection, that relate to task-disruptive behavior include the needs for cognitive clarity and for consensual validation. Situations that are ambiguous and lacking structure make such needs salient. Pupils often react to such situations by seeking structure through excessive dependency on the teacher, or by discovering how other pupils are structuring the situation. Much of the questioning and surreptitious talking that occurs in these situations appears to be in response to these needs. Similar reactions occur when the teacher is perceived to be unfair. This sudden departure from the rules often produces consternation and subsequent attempts to rectify the situation, to return it to a condition of predictability. For example, an unresolved playground incident where the teacher was unfair may interfere with a subsequent classroom task.

The buildup of tension related to frustrated and ignored social needs during task activities, along with the increasing costs of task

---

32. R. Schmuck, "Some Relationships of Peer Liking Patterns in the Classroom to Pupil Attitudes and Achievement," *The School Review*, Vol. 71, No. 3 (1963), pp. 337–59.

activity due to fatigue, boredom, and so on, makes it impossible for the teacher to maintain indefinitely a sustained level of task activity. Inevitably the forces in favor of non-task activities become strong enough to shift energies in the non-task direction. Thus, a rhythm of alternation between task and non-task activities can be observed in most task groups.

Much of what has been said in this chapter is relevant to one of the oldest social psychological issues in the history of educational research. Since the pioneering work of Lewin, Lippitt, and White,[33] much has been written about the relative advantages of two different styles of teacher leadership.[34] While a variety of terms have been applied to two polar methods of teaching since their original designation as democratic and authoritarian, the contrast for the most part has been between the leader who is accepting, permissive, considerate, and person-oriented and the one who is directive, controlling, and task-oriented. In educational research the terms *learner-centered* or *pupil-centered* climate and *teacher-centered* climate have frequently been used to label these two types. While a pupil-centered climate is repeatedly referred to as ideal, the research evidence has not consistently favored one over the other. Today researchers realize that the relative effectiveness of each climate depends on the nature of the task, the personality and skills of all group members, and the group structure. Particularly important is the leader's position in the group structure. These facts can be understood by noting the manner in which features of the task, the structure of the group, and the personalities of its members affect their rewards and costs.

The preceding section emphasized the role of rewards and costs in determining conformity to group norms. To the extent that task activity is satisfying, the group will be productive. We have already noted that identification with the teacher establishes norms that are congruent with his values, enhancing his legitimate power. Unfortunately, research and theory suggest elements in both the democratic and authoritarian styles of leadership that foster identification. The democratic teacher, more concerned with the socioemo-

33. K. Lewin, R. Lippitt, and R. K. White, "Patterns of Aggressive Behavior in Experimentally Created Social Climates," *Journal of Social Psychology*, Vol. 10 (1939), pp. 271–99.
34. J. Whithall and W. W. Lewis, "Social Interaction in the Classroom," in N. L. Gage, ed., *Handbook of Research on Teaching* (Chicago: Rand McNally, 1963).

tional needs of the child, is the target of more intense liking, which facilitates identification. At the same time, the greater power and status of the autocratic teacher similarly stimulates identification.

Perhaps a role which includes social distance to maintain respect and yet gives some attention to satisfying the socioemotional needs of the followers is optimal. This should not only maximize teacher influence on the normative climate but, since it contributes to group satisfaction, the power of the group to enforce its norms should be increased. One element in the democratic style of leadership that favors productivity in many situations is increased pupil participation. Assuming that such participation leads to the formulation of norms and goals favoring task excellence, the process of participation generates forces maximizing motivation toward conformity and goal achievement.

To the degree that intrinsic satisfaction in the task area is increased, one would expect more task activity. A democratic style of leadership may increase the intrinsic rewards of task activity by allowing for self-fulfillment, increased status, and so on and thus stimulate task activity. At the same time this leadership style may be a source of additional cost to group members. Where group members are unable to cope with the demands of the task, or where they feel a lack of sufficient structure in the situation, or, finally, where they think that it is the leader's task and not theirs to provide direction, the frustration that results from a democratic leadership style may motivate a withdrawal from task activities and movement into a variety of non-task areas.[35] Personality variables appear to be influential here. Structured teaching procedures, in contrast with those of a more unstructured nature, have been shown to be associated with better performance for highly compulsive children.[36] In the same study, children with high anxiety performed less well than those with less anxiety in classes using less structured teaching methods. Effective control may be necessary to marshal effectively group resources in the direction of goal achievement in any classroom. Group decisions which merely reflect the will of the majority may be defective on two grounds. First, they may be technically deficient because important elements in a minority's solution have not

35. B. H. Raven and J. Rietsema, "The Effects of Varied Clarity of Group Goal and Group Path upon the Individual and His Relation to His Group," *Human Relations,* Vol. 10 (1957), pp. 29–45.

36. J. W. Grimes and W. Allensmith, "Compulsivity, Anxiety, and School Achievement," *Merrill-Palmer Quarterly,* Vol. 7 (1961), pp. 247–69.

been included. Second, the majority may need minority aid to carry out their decisions. Decisions that ignore the view of a minority result in a dissident subgroup and are apt not to be effectively implemented.

Implications for the Classroom

We have suggested that the balance of task to non-task activities in the classroom is greatly influenced by the relevance of each activity to the satisfactions experienced by students. To the extent that task compared to non-task activity is intrinsically rewarding, related to important goals, and associated with group and self-administered rewards, the learning process is facilitated. Although there are limits in the extent to which activities can be made intrinsically rewarding, and related to important goals, group- and self-administered rewards are too often overlooked as a source of support for an activity.

If the teacher can marshal group forces in support of task activities, his own effectiveness is considerably augmented. He can do this if he can alter the normative climate of the class in a direction favorable to task activities and if he can modify the classroom group structure so as to maximize conformity. At times this may require breaking up subgroups within the classroom whose normative climates favor non-task activities. At other times these groups may be left intact, and by working through the more influential students, the teacher can marshal group forces in support of task activities.

The organization of task activities should also be kept in mind. Such activities as group projects that require cooperative effort are apt to stimulate a normative climate favoring task excellence, since the satisfactions of each student are dependent on the contribution of all. It is important to integrate each child into the group, to insure that favorable normative forces have maximum effect on a child, and also to insure that the child's socioemotional needs are sufficiently met so as to avoid disruptive behavior or withdrawal.

Finally, teachers should be selected to exemplify values conducive to educational excellence. They should have the characteristics and resources that maximize identification of the student with them, thus giving them optimal influence over the student.

Chapter Six

The Role
of the Teacher

In this chapter we use current role theory to organize what is known about the role of the school and college teacher. Central to role theory is the concept of *role strain,* the varying degrees of difficulty that persons experience in carrying out their occupational and other social roles. The concept of role strain is useful in understanding human interaction in many contexts; it facilitates the translation of abstract concepts of interaction into the daily experience of persons. It is when persons have difficulty in meeting role expectations that they become aware of the impact of these social processes on their lives. Role strain is also crucial to practical concerns. How well teachers perform and how satisfied they are in this role have important consequences for the achievement of the purposes or functions within the educational enterprise.

In the following discussion, we analyze role strain and its resolution on three familiar levels: the social system, the personality dynamics of the individual, and the cultural system.

SOCIAL SYSTEM VARIABLES AND ROLE STRAIN

At the outset we may distinguish several general features of systems of expectations related to role strain.

Role Consensus. The degree to which system participants agree on the requirements of a social role is termed role consensus. Where there is lack of agreement, difficulties are apt to arise. If some teachers believe they are obligated to participate in a variety of community service activities and other teachers do not, they are apt to experience difficulty in developing agreed-upon means of protecting themselves against excessive demands from this source.

116

Similarly, if a teacher defines as a prerogative of his role the right to participate in curriculum planning, but his principal does not, curriculum decisions may be accompanied by considerable strain.

These examples also illustrate the distinction commonly drawn between *intraposition consensus* and *interposition consensus*. Our first example, involving a difference in expectations between persons occupying the *same* position or role category, illustrates a departure from intraposition consensus. Our second, involving disagreement between occupants of two different positions or *role partners,* illustrates a departure from interposition consensus.

Although the illustrations given here have an "all or none" quality, often disagreement on role expectations is a matter of degree. One person may feel that a given right or obligation is mandatory, while another feels that it is merely preferable. A teacher, for instance, may feel that he must be consulted regarding a curriculum change; his principal may feel that although such consultation is preferable it is not mandatory. Finally, participants not only have expectations regarding the *behavior* of a person in a social role; they also have ideas concerning what personal attributes go with the role. Teachers are expected to possess a variety of stereotyped physical, social, and personality characteristics. Consensus may vary with respect to these role attributes as well.

Intraposition Consensus. Expectations regarding the teacher role held by his role partners—student, principal, and parent—vary considerably among individuals within each category of partner. A study of expectations held by citizens of a Midwestern city reports that almost one-fourth of the sample thought that the teacher must or should give special attention to weak students even when this slows down class progress.[1] At the same time, slightly over one-half thought that he should not or must not do so. Other studies indicate that teachers themselves show considerable variations in their role conceptions.

Most studies bearing on consensus regarding the role of the teacher are concerned with interposition consensus. The few studies that provide data on intrapositional consensus provide little basis

---

1. Clinton Snyder, "General and Specific Role Expectations for Teachers," unpublished manuscript, Michigan State University. Cited in W. B. Brookover and D. Gottlieb, *A Sociology of Education* (New York: American Book Co., 1964).

for inferring with confidence the reasons why consensus varies.[2] We can only present some general principles, drawn from a theory of conformity,[3] which are consistent with some of the empirical findings.

Shared expectations most often arise in those areas of behavior most critically related to the reward-cost outcomes persons experience from a given relation. As we previously noted, reward-cost outcomes consist of the gratification and frustration experienced by persons in interaction. Further, to the degree that their outcomes are vitally affected by the behavior in question, conformity pressures will ensure maximum consensus. For example, because they do not receive an income comparable to their investment in education and training, despite the importance in our society of an adequate income, teachers hold almost unanimously the expectation that they should be paid more for their services. Also consistent with this principle is the greater intraposition consensus for teachers on role items drawn from the personal, family, and social recreational area than on those from the civic, political, and religious areas.[4] In view of the contemporary importance of personal, family, and social-recreational interactions and of the traditional restrictions in these areas for teachers, it could be argued that strongly supported norms would develop in this area. On the whole, however, the few items upon which investigators report intraposition consensus do not vary sufficiently in reward-cost outcomes to test adequately this principle, and our discussion here must be regarded as speculative.

A further limitation of the studies on intraposition consensus is that little is known of the consequences of disagreement concerning role expectations. While it is logical that role strain should arise from this source, the forms that it takes and the consequences ensuing need to be investigated further. With few exceptions, however, the research literature does show that marked role consensus is associated with member satisfaction, both in educational and other

---

2. Snyder, *op. cit.;* L. V. Manwiller, "Expectations Regarding Teachers," *Journal of Experimental Education,* Vol. 26 (1958), pp. 315–54; C. E. Fishburn, "Teacher Role Perception in the Secondary School," *Journal of Teacher Education,* Vol. 13 (1962), pp. 55–59.

3. P. F. Secord and C. W. Backman, *Social Psychology* (New York: McGraw-Hill, 1964).

4. Manwiller, *op. cit.*

institutional settings.[5] But the effects on performance of both the individual and the work unit have yet to be adequately documented. One study of agricultural-science teachers does conclude that consensus is positively related to both satisfaction and effective performance.[6] However, the investigators' method of measuring intraposition consensus and the fact that the persons compared did not constitute functioning groups leave us in some doubt whether their findings may be applied to intraposition consensus as we define it.

Interposition Consensus. Compared with intraposition consensus, more research is available on agreement among the teacher's role partners. Perhaps the most extensive study has been that of Biddle, Rosencranz, and Rankin.[7] These investigators compared the conceptions of the teacher role held by four groups: teachers, school officials, parents, and students. The greatest overall agreement concerning the role of teacher occurred between school officials and teachers. The greatest disagreement existed between the role conceptions held by teachers and those held by pupils. The role conceptions of parents were intermediate, closer to that of the teacher than those of the pupils but more distant than that of school officials.

Two hypotheses that had been previously advanced to explain role consensus were only partly supported by these data.[8] It had been suggested that the greater the frequency of interaction between role partners, the greater would be the resultant consensus. This principle is consistent with the higher agreement between school officials and teachers compared with agreement between parents and teachers. However, it fails to explain why pupils, who have the greatest amount of interaction with the teacher, disagree most with his conception of his role. A second principle, that of common back-

---

5. D. H. Jenkins and R. Lippitt, *Interpersonal Perceptions of Teachers, Students, and Parents* (Washington, D.C.: National Education Association, 1951); N. Gross, W. S. Mason, and A. W. McEachern, *Explorations in Role Analysis* (New York: Wiley, 1958); R. L. Kahn, D. M. Wolfe, R. P. Quinn, J. D. Snoek, and R. A. Rosenthal, *Organizational Stress* (New York: Wiley, 1964).
6. B. L. Bible and J. D. McComas, "Role Consensus and Teacher Effectiveness," *Social Forces*, Vol. 42 (1963), pp. 225–32.
7. B. J. Biddle, H. A. Rosencranz, and E. F. Rankin, "Studies in the Role of the Public School Teacher" (Columbia: University of Missouri Press, 1961).
8. Gross, Mason, and McEachern, *op. cit.*

ground, fares much better. With the exception of school board members, school officials are for the most part ex-teachers and thus are more similar in background to teachers than are parents or pupils. Further, by virtue of age, teachers are more similar in background and experience to parents than to pupils.

Both of these principles have been combined into a general principle of social distance, which has been advanced to explain variation in role accuracy and conformity.[9] It could be applied equally well to variations in role consensus. To the extent that persons frequently interact and have similar attitudes and values, they are apt to influence each other's conceptions in the direction of consensus. This principle, termed the *social distance hypothesis* by Green and Biddle, is consistent with the data if we assume that the marked lack of consensus between pupil and teacher regarding role expectations occurs because the sharp differences in their attitude toward school work and toward play prevent them from mutually influencing each other. However, additional evidence is inconsistent with the social distance hypothesis. It has been shown that close personal relations between male teachers and their nonteacher neighbors do not materially affect the neighbors' conceptions of the role of the male teacher in the direction of consensus.[10]

Our previously stated principle that group consensus depends upon reward-cost outcomes is also consistent with these findings regarding consensus for different role partners. It has the further advantage of making some sense of the specific areas of disagreement. Any particular action of a teacher is apt to produce similar outcomes for both teacher and school official, but an opposite outcome for the student. For example, a teacher who fails a student who has performed poorly is upholding the standards of the school and will be supported by the principal. But this action is costly to the pupil. Since the outcomes of the parent are similar in part to those of the pupil and in part to those of the teacher and school official, parents would be expected to agree with them only in part.

These differences in consensus become clearer when we examine the areas of disagreement about the role of the teacher held by his role partners. Most obviously in support of this principle are findings that teachers, parents, and school officials expect and approve

---

9. P. F. Green and B. J. Biddle, personal communication to the authors, 1964.
10. Snyder, *op. cit.*

of more supervision of pupils by teachers than do pupils, and that teachers to a greater extent than these other groups disapprove of teachers doing menial tasks. Less obviously relevant are findings which suggest that parents expect teachers to engage in more maintenance of order, more control of deviant behavior, and more supervision outside the classroom and to speak out more frequently at PTA meetings than the teachers themselves believe is appropriate. These role items all involve additional demands on the teacher that adversely affect the rewards and costs experienced in his role.

Further support for the principle that group consensus depends on the common relevance of acts for the outcomes of role partners is found in studies on interposition consensus within a particular sector of the teacher role. In a study of the relative importance attributed to facets of the teacher role, considerable disagreement was found between teachers and administrators in two high schools.[11] Whereas administrators rated as most important the function of "acting as a liaison between school and community," teachers rated this function as least important. Teachers, in turn, rated "mediator of the culture" as most important, a function which the administrators rated as least important. "Director of learning" was ranked second in importance by teachers and fifth in importance by administrators. "Member of a profession" was ranked next to the most important facet of the teacher role by administrators and next to the least important facet by teachers. Again, if we assume that role perceptions are biased in a direction that increases rewards and reduces costs of each role partner, at least some of these differences make sense. A major concern of the administrator is school-community relations. This would lead him to emphasize aspects of the teacher role relevant to this function. On the other hand, the teacher's main concern is his instructional function, hence his emphasis on his role as "mediator of the culture" and "director of learning."

A primary concern for the instructional role on the part of the teacher and emphasis on school-community relations on the part of the administrator may also underlie the marked difference reported [12] between teachers and school officials (principals and superintendents) in responses to the item, "When a student's passing or

---

11. Fishburn, *op. cit.*
12. Melvin Seeman, "Role Conflict and Ambivalence in Leadership," *American Sociological Review,* Vol. 18 (1953), pp. 371–78.

failing is doubtful, do you think an ideal superintendent should (1) leave the decision up to the teacher or (2) pretty much take the responsibility for the final decision?" Among teachers, 80 percent chose the first alternative, while only 40 percent of the principals and superintendents did so. The school official's preference for the second alternative could be interpreted as reflecting concern for school-community relations, particularly in the small community investigated in this study.

Research on the ideal or popular traits of teachers, students, and parents provides further support for this interpretation.[13] College teachers ranked intelligence first in their descriptions of the ideal student, while students ranked this trait fourth. Further, in their description of the ideal professor, students ranked understanding first and professors rated this fourth. Among junior high school students, attributes liked by pupils in both parents and teachers revolved around the power which these adults exercised over the pupils. Parents' conceptions of teachers seemed to be largely influenced by the teachers' relation to their child as it influenced the child's school achievement. As we have noted elsewhere, the parents' satisfaction depends strongly on their children's school performance. Teachers' conceptions of both parents and students appeared to be greatly influenced by a desire for friendly relations. The need for emotional support and acceptance, which we discuss later, appears to be a particularly strong and relatively unmet need for many teachers.

Role Conflict. The term "role conflict" has been employed in social psychology to describe situations where persons in a role category are exposed to incompatible expectations. Incompatibility may take the form of conflict or competition. In the former the expectations are such that meeting one expectation makes it impossible to honor the other. The teacher who gives special attention to the poorer student at the expense of class progress meets the expectations of some in the community but violates the expectations of others.[14] In the case of competition, honoring one expectation competes in time and energy with honoring the other. School super-

13. Anita Yourglich, "Study on Correlations Between College Teachers' and Students' Concepts of 'Ideal Student' and 'Ideal Teacher,'" *Journal of Educational Research,* Vol. 49 (1955), pp. 59–64; Jenkins and Lippitt, *op. cit.*
14. Brookover and Gottlieb, *op. cit.*

intendents are expected by teachers to work for adequate school financing, including teacher salary increases.[15] This necessitates spending time with community leaders, preparing budget justifications, and so on. At the same time, teachers expect superintendents to spend time with them, consulting, visiting classrooms, and so forth. With just so many hours in a day most superintendents find it difficult to meet both of these sets of expectations.

Incompatible expectations may exist within a given sector or between sectors of a role and may be held by a position incumbent, one or more of his role partners, or both. The role conflict of the school superintendent is an example of role incompatibility within a sector, that sector involving his relations with teachers. Both he and his role partner, the teacher, hold expectations which compete with each other. The teacher who is expected by his pupils to engage in less supervision and by his superintendent in more supervision of pupils is exposed to conflicting demands from different sectors of his role, one sector consisting of the expectations of his pupils and the other originating with his superintendent.

While lack of consensus on role expectations may underlie role conflict, it is not the only source. The person, his fellow position occupants, and various role partners may all agree on the appropriate expectations in a given situation, but the teacher may still be subject to incompatible expectations. Both schoolteachers and superintendents agree that it is desirable for the latter to achieve and maintain adequate teacher salaries and to work closely with the teacher in the classroom. Yet, to do both is difficult. Probably no social system is so well organized that the participants do not experience some strain; however, a variety of features of the social systems within which the teacher functions conspire to make his role more stressful than that of many other role incumbents. To these we now turn.

Role Set Articulation. If we examine the expectations relevant to the relation that the teacher has with each of his role partners—pupils, parents, and administrators—we may note certain sources of competition and conflict. These arise because of a lack of articulation in the system of expectations confronting the teacher. A perfectly articulated system would be so organized that the role occu-

---

15. Seeman, *op. cit.*

pants would not experience strain from conflicting or competing expectations. This might be accomplished in several ways: (1) if conflicting expectations are excluded from the system, (2) if built-in mechanisms prevent a person from being exposed to conflicting and competing expectations at the same time, or (3) if strain-free methods of resolution are provided. Elsewhere we have detailed such mechanisms.[16] In the discussion which follows we will concentrate on sources of conflicting and competing expectations, first with respect to the same type of role partner and then between different types.

Within-Sector Sources of Strain. The teacher as a leader of pupils in the learning process shares with other leadership roles a basic source of strain in the incompatibility between instrumental and socioemotional leadership. Most leaders are confronted with the task of directing their followers toward goal achievement and at the same time creating a group situation that allows for the satisfaction of their own and their followers' socioemotional needs. In many instances behavior appropriate to meeting the first function interferes with carrying out the second. In the case of the teacher, various pressures which he exerts on the student in the direction of classroom achievement conflict or at least compete with gratification of the students' socioemotional needs. This dilemma is a basic source of the emergence in most work groups of an informal structure of relations, frequently opposed in certain respects to the formal structure since it arises in response to socioemotional needs whose fulfillment is interfered with by the formal structure. In the classroom, much conflict between pupil and teacher arises in this connection. The problem of teacher control is magnified to the extent that students gratify their socioemotional needs (whispering, "horsing around," passing notes) at the expense of meeting the demands imposed by the teacher for instrumental achievement, learning.

While this conflict is inherent in any leadership role, its intensity varies in part with the degree to which the leader emphasizes one function and the followers the other. In the school situation this appears to differ by grade. Children in the early grades find considerable socioemotional support at home and are more accepting of adult definitions of the school situation. At the same time, the

---

16. Secord and Backman, *op. cit.*

elementary teacher generally expects less diligence from and is more solicitous of the total needs of the child. These combined factors should minimize conflict between the two aspects of the leadership role. The adolescent emancipating himself from the home and seeking new socioemotional support in the peer group is more apt to emphasize satisfaction of socioemotional needs in his definition of the school situation. But the high school teacher confronting this student emphasizes the instrumental function, creating a greater problem for himself in carrying out the leadership role.

While the college teacher emphasizes task leadership to an even greater degree, the college student is not only older but is typically from social groups that emphasize the task function of teaching. Hence, the difference is marked between the climates of high school and college classrooms. Whereas the former is often fraught with an undercurrent of strife which produces considerable strain for both teacher and student, the latter may be so placid as to be somewhat boring.

Occasional variations in climate from school to school at the same grade level may sometimes be explained in terms of the dual function of the teacher as task and socioemotional leader. Teachers' experience of strain undoubtedly reflects the differing emphasis which students and teachers at each school place on these two facets of the teacher role. For instance, students in schools in lower-class areas are apt to be in greater disagreement with the teacher in valuing task and socioemotional activities than students from middle-class schools. Classrooms also vary within the same school in their emphasis on these two functions and in the extent to which the teacher is able to integrate these two facets of his role. He may attempt to emphasize one or the other, become the hard taskmaster and feared disciplinarian or, in the college parlance, become "a good Joe." Ideally he may, if he has the appropriate personality and skill and if luck provides him with a receptive class, attempt to blend the two, offering a combination of psychological rewards that includes both satisfaction of achievement and socioemotional needs in exchange for a satisfactory level of task performance.

A related source of strain which the teacher role has in common with other leadership roles revolves around the handling of emotional involvement with students. His instrumental role includes not only motivating and directing the learning process but also certifying competency. Both are accomplished, in part at least, through periodic assessment and grading of the student. The accomplishment of this facet of his role is facilitated by affective neutrality. To the degree that he neither likes nor dislikes a student he will be able to meet the role obligation to grade students impartially. At the same time, to the degree that he attempts to meet the socioemotional needs of his students, he runs the risk of emotional involvement. When this occurs he may face sanctions from others as well as from himself for departing from strict impartiality. This dilemma is inherent in the demands of his students and his other role partners that he be both warm and friendly and yet have no "pets."

A related problem revolves around the conflict between the teacher's expectations for pupil achievement and the expectations that pupil and parent often hold for special treatment.[17] A number of studies have documented the tendency of teachers to be influenced by the social-class origin of the child in the grades he gives and the rewards and punishments he imposes.[18] A professional ideology that emphasizes competitive achievement may in many instances be a source of guilt and consequent strain. Given the fact that other role partners, including students, can exert sanctions when his behavior departs from their expectations, he often is faced with either giving up professional standards or accepting abuse from students and parents.

So far our comments have been largely relevant to the teacher-pupil sector of the teacher role. Many elements of strain in the teacher-pupil sector are reflected in the parent-teacher sector because of strong bonds of empathy between parent and child. Hence, both the child and his parents may be distressed if they believe the teacher has not evaluated his performance fairly. Because among middle-class Americans the child's behavior is thought to reflect the quality of his upbringing, however, parents are apt to have higher expectations for their child's achievement than he does himself.

More unique to the parent-teacher relation, however, are strains arising from differences regarding the extent of teacher authority and responsibility in the socialization of the child. While both

---

17. C. W. Gordon, "The Role of the Teacher in the Social Structure of the High School," *Journal of Educational Sociology*, Vol. 29 (1955), pp. 21–29; *The Social System of the High School: A Study in the Sociology of Adolescence* (New York: Macmillan, 1957).

18. W. L. Warner, R. J. Havighurst and M. B. Loeb, *Who Shall Be Educated?* (New York: Harper & Row, 1944); A. B. Hollingshead, *Elmtown's Youth* (New York: Wiley, 1949); Gordon, "The Role of the Teacher in the Social Structure of the High School."

teacher and parent may agree that the child should learn the three R's, the degree to which the teacher may educate "the whole child" may be in dispute. Sex education and lessons bearing on political or religious issues are sample areas of dispute. Parents and teachers may also disagree on the forms of discipline which the teacher may legitimately apply. Whether corporal punishment may be employed and by whom and under what circumstances it may be employed is still an unsettled question in many school systems.

Our previous discussion of disparities in definition of the teacher's role between teacher and school officials suggests other sources of strain. What the school official regards as appropriate teacher behavior is greatly influenced by his orientation toward the school board and the community. Behavior that creates difficulties between the school and parents or other influential community members is viewed in a markedly different light by school officials and teachers. Administrators expect the teacher to emphasize his function as a liaison between the school and the community, but teachers give minimal priority to this aspect of their role and maximum priority to their professional function of instruction. Thus, strain may arise to the extent that parents and other community members disagree with the teacher's judgment concerning the content of what they teach or the methods they use in teaching.

In summary, an examination of the relation between teachers and each of their major role partners (pupils, parents, school officials) suggests that a basic source of strain is that these partners in interaction have different goals; hence a given act by one partner will have different outcomes for the others, facilitating gratification of the needs of one and frustrating the needs of the other. Where this is the case relations are likely to be strained.

Social System Articulation. We may look at the teacher as a participant in a number of social systems besides those involving his occupational role. He is a family member and a citizen of his community. Certain occupational roles—teacher, physician, minister, movie star, and politician—carry expectations that extend beyond the occupational duties themselves and conflict with family, citizen, and other roles of the individual. Getzels and Guba report two examples of this kind of conflict experienced by teachers:

> 1. *The socioeconomic role.* In most communities teachers are assumed to be members of at least a quasi-professional group for whom middle-class standards of living are expected. However, in comparison

with persons for whom similar standards are required, the teacher receives remuneration inadequate for conforming to these expectations. Many of the specific strains felt by the teachers could be traced to this conflict, arising not alone because they are underpaid, but also because they are expected to maintain standards of tastes and living which are out of reach in terms of the salaries they receive.

2. *The citizen role.* The adult members of a community are generally assumed to be responsible citizens whose judgment regarding their own conduct may be trusted. The teacher, however, is frequently not granted the same confidence with respect to his public and private conduct. He may, for example, be required to participate with more vigor in church affairs than are his neighbors, but with less vigor in political matters than his own beliefs (or for that matter, good citizenship) require. Thus, although the teacher resides in the community, his citizenship may be only second class, since the expectations placed upon him in his role as teacher restrict the freedom of his role as citizen.[19]

These conflicts arise because of the diffuse and pervasive character of the teacher role. Relatively large areas of his behavior are restricted by role expectations. Numerous studies have documented the fact that the standards set for teacher conduct far exceed those specified for other occupational groups, with the exception of the clergy.[20] In part, this may be a product of community concern over the teacher role in the socialization of young children; in part, however, it appears to be related to the altruistic character of this role and the classification of the teacher as a public servant. These two features require further comment.

First, just as roles differ in diffuseness, they also differ in the degree to which position occupants may satisfy their individual needs at the expense of their role partners. Those in the so-called "helping professions" such as social work are expected to place their clients' welfare above the satisfaction of their own needs. Others, such as businessmen, are not expected to necessarily do so. The teacher falls toward the "helping profession" end of the continuum of roles. He is expected to place the welfare of the child and of the community above the satisfaction of his own needs. To illustrate, even many teachers would regard a teacher strike for higher salaries

19. J. W. Getzels and E. G. Guba, "The Structure of Roles and Role Conflict in the Teaching Situation," *Journal of Educational Sociology*, Vol. 29 (1955), pp. 30–40.
20. L. A. Cook, *Community Background of Education* (New York: McGraw-Hill, 1938); Florence Greenhoe, "The Community Contacts and Participation of 9,122 Public School Teachers Selected as a National Sample," *School and Society*, Vol. 50 (1939), pp. 510–12.

as inappropriate or unprofessional conduct. Related to this are expectations related to his "public servant" role. The vast majority of teachers are in the public school system. As employees of the community they are subject to many demands not made of other occupational groups. Not only does this support the diffuse and altruistic character of the role, but it also undoubtedly accounts for such expectations as the one which specifies that he live and buy in the community which employs him.

Second, the degree to which restrictive role expectations emerge and are maintained reflects in part the degree to which they are effectively resisted by teachers. Such resistance depends on how strongly motivated they are to resist encroachments on their rights as private citizens and on their power relative to the power of other role partners. The fact that the teaching role has been secondary for many undoubtedly has affected the motivation to resist role definitions that interfere with teaching satisfaction. For many young women, teaching is a temporary occupation until marriage and motherhood, and for many married women, teaching is subordinate to their family roles. Further, the lack of more attractive occupational alternatives for women undoubtedly lowers motivation to resist limitations on adult freedoms that are part of the role of the teacher. Finally, as we will explain more fully in a later section, women in general and teachers in particular tend to be more heavily socialized toward conservatism; hence a woman teacher resents restrictions on her conduct less than would male teachers or persons in many other occupational groups.

The Articulation of the Reward System. Social systems must be organized so that the behavior of the various role partners results in level of reward sufficient to motivate persons to remain in the system and to adequately portray their roles. We have already noted that the teaching role is likely to provide inadequate rewards. This is so not only in salaries but also in the satisfaction of socioemotional needs. Researchers found that teachers strongly desired friendly relations with parents and pupils, but these role partners appeared to be unaware of this need of the teacher.[21]

What is perceived as an adequate reward depends on two related principles—*distributive justice* and *status congruency*. Occupational

---

21. Jenkins and Lippitt, *op. cit.*

roles may be ranked on a number of dimensions such as the pay received, the amount of education or training required, or the responsibility of the position. These are examples of rewards, investments, and costs, respectively. *Distributive justice* is obtained for a position when the rewards accorded the position occupants minus the costs which they incur are proportional to their investments. Many teachers feel that the rewards received, particularly the monetary ones, are out of line with their investments, since typically their pay is considerably below that obtained by professionals with similar educational investments. Further, the teaching profession has long been a classic example of *status incongruency*. This occurs where the person or position is ranked differently relative to various attributes. The teacher, compared to other occupational groups, ranks high on the dimension of education but low on the dimension of salary. Departures from the principles of distributive justice and status congruency have been associated with behavior reflecting role strain.[22]

CULTURAL VARIABLES AND ROLE STRAIN

So far in this chapter we have been concerned with the system of expectations that role partners share in varying degrees regarding each other's behavior. Related to these expectations are the wider belief systems shared by persons with a common culture. Just as one can talk of the degree to which a social system is articulated, one can speak of various degrees of articulation within the belief systems of a culture. To the degree that various beliefs in a culture are inconsistent with one another, persons sharing them experience strain. This may be aggravated further where individuals in the culture differ in their acceptance of these beliefs. Finally, to the degree that articulation is imperfect between the cultural system and the social system, persons are apt to experience strain: they find themselves exposed to expectations that lead to behavior contrary to their beliefs.

In American culture one can note a number of inconsistencies between elements of belief relevant to the educational process in

22. Gerhard Lenski, "Status Crystallization: A Nonvertical Dimension of Social Status," *American Sociological Review,* Vol. 19 (1954), pp. 405–13; R. V. Exline and R. C. Ziller, "Status Congruency and Interpersonal Conflict in Decision-Making Groups," *Human Relations,* Vol. 12 (1959), pp. 147–62.

general and to the role of the teacher in particular. Fundamental to many inconsistencies in American beliefs regarding education is the conflict between our democratic ideology, with its emphasis on *equality* of individuals, and our worship of individual accomplishment, with its emphasis on *competitive* achievement. In a society that emphasizes both of these a basic dilemma arises in those areas where individual differences, denied or minimized by the popular doctrines of equality, do in fact make a difference in the competitive process. This is certainly the case in education. The basic dilemma is one of handling failure and its demoralizing effects on the individual. For if all are really equal, then to achieve less than one's fellows could be interpreted as moral failure. One solution to this dilemma is to devalue success in those areas where one is likely to fall short. This, we suggest, is the root of the ambivalence regarding educational success in American society. Children are expected by parents and others to try to succeed in the educational process, but if they fall short this is not too important because, they rationalize, education is not, after all, that important. "After all," the saying goes, "a lot of people have done quite well without it." This ambivalence toward educational success spreads to the teacher, who, compared to the general population, has been somewhat more successful in this area. This success, as well as the role itself, is a target of ambivalence. It is all right to be smart but not to be *too* smart. Persons with too much schooling are popularly thought to suffer a number of incapacities. It is false but common folklore that persons with high intelligence have high rates of mental illness, that college professors are absent-minded and impractical, and so on.

This opposition between the doctrine of equality and emphasis on achievement underlies other ideological conflicts as well. Those who believe in upgrading the schools and in emphasizing academic fundamentals are opposed by those who believe that the curriculum should be broadened to meet the needs of students at all levels of ability. Cutting across this belief controversy is the conflict between philosophies of education which emphasize educating the "whole child" and those which mainly emphasize the child's academic skills.

Teaching methods in the public school have also been plagued by conflicting belief elements. The proponents of progressive education and those labeled traditionalists have long differed over matters of curriculum and method. While it is not our purpose to examine these conflicting elements in detail, they do have relevance to the strains teachers experience.

Differing belief systems underlie the conflicting expectations of teachers, parents, school officials, and others and account in part for the lack of consensus that we have observed. Teachers frequently find themselves in a position where their behavior, while perhaps consistent with some elements of their beliefs, is contrary to others. Finally, the various ambivalent feelings toward educational achievement not only contribute to his problem of motivating the student to excel, but also undoubtedly create problems in maintaining a favorable self concept. These problems will be dealt with in more detail in the section which follows.

PERSONALITY AND ROLE STRAIN

By personality and temperament, an individual may or may not be well suited to a social role. To the extent that the demands of the role are incompatible with personality traits and needs, role strain occurs. Studies have demonstrated that a person selects roles that allow him to behave in a manner compatible with his personality.[23] This selection process is important in the decisions that eventually lead a person to become a teacher. A comparison of the personality characteristics of the public school teacher in American society with the requirements of the role suggests a close fit at most points, although a few aspects of the role produce strain.

Although many studies, some very extensive, have been directed toward identifying the personality, attitudes, and values of the teacher, all too often such studies have not compared teachers with nonteachers. This is essential; personality-trait profiles from tests or other assessment devices mean little unless these profiles can be compared with other known groups, especially nonteachers. Acceptable alternatives are to compare college seniors who are education majors with seniors in other fields or to compare seniors who plan to take graduate work leading to specific career choices, including teaching. Several extensive studies of this kind agree in characterizing prospective teachers as more "people-oriented" than nonteachers. In a survey of over 33,000 college seniors shortly before

---

23. C. W. Backman and P. F. Secord, "The Self and Role Selection," in C. Gordon and K. J. Gergen, eds., *The Self in Social Interaction* (New York: Wiley, 1968).

their graduation in June 1961, Davis found that 70 percent of those choosing education as a career preferred to "work with people rather than things." [24] This proportion was surpassed only by students choosing nursing, social work, and clinical psychology. In contrast, less than 20 percent of the seniors choosing such fields as physics, chemistry, and engineering checked this item. Results similar to these were obtained in an earlier study.[25]

Consistent with these findings are other reports that male education students have high social interests,[26] that teachers score higher than the norms on personality traits such as sociability, friendliness, and personal relations,[27] and that college seniors shifting to science teaching score higher on social interests, sociability, and personal relations than those seniors continuing in science.[28]

This "people-oriented" characteristic of teachers seems to fit rather well the role of teacher. Not only does his work require him to establish friendly relations with and to get to know and understand his pupils, but he must be able to get along with parents who visit him concerning their children's progress.

We have referred earlier to the teacher role as one that demands conformity and conventionality, not only in the classroom itself but even in the teacher's private life. Parents, principals, superintendents, and school board members are especially sensitive to any suggestion that a teacher's behavior does not conform closely to society's mores and are apt to make their disapproval known when they encounter deviant actions. Such constraints are attractive only to the individual who is relatively docile and conformist: they repel the rebel and the individualist. That teachers as a group are indeed conformists is well testified to by the research literature briefly reviewed below.

Davis found that, to a greater extent than any other group except nursing seniors, education seniors described themselves as "con-

24. J. A. Davis, *Great Aspirations* (Chicago: Aldine, 1964).
25. Morris Rosenberg, *Occupations and Values* (New York: Macmillan, 1957).
26. M. S. MacLean, M. S. Gowan, and J. C. Gowan, "A Teacher Selection and Counseling Service," *Journal of Educational Research*, Vol. 48 (1955), pp. 669–77.
27. J. C. Gowan and M. S. Gowan, "The Guilford-Zimmerman and the California Psychological Inventory in the Measurement of Teaching Candidates," *California Journal of Educational Research*, Vol. 6 (1955), pp. 35–37.
28. E. C. Lee, "Career Development of Science Teachers," *Journal of Research in Science Teaching*, Vol. 1 (1963), pp. 54–63.

ventional in opinions and values." [29] In 1943 Strong reported the responses of 238 female elementary school teachers to the Vocational Interest Blank.[30] Compared with adult women in general, they indicated that, to a greater extent, they liked religious people, fashionably dressed people, teetotalers, and thrifty people and that they disliked irreligious people, unconventional people, women who smoke, carelessly dressed people, foreigners, political independents, and people who take chances. These responses clearly suggest conventional, socially conservative attitudes on the part of this teacher group from an earlier generation.

Evidence from the Minnesota Multiphasic Personality Inventory is consistent with this emphasis on conventionality. While many studies fail to show consistent deviations for teachers on any of the clinical scales, several studies agree in reporting an unusually high "K" score for teachers and education students.[31] The K scale was developed as a measure of test-taking attitude: a high score represents a denial of personal inadequacies, of abnormalities, of emotional instability, and of criticism of other persons. Thus Gowan concludes that, to a greater extent than the average individual, teachers are responsible, conscientious, conforming, and friendly and that they emphasize control of self and adaptation to the needs and demands of others.[32]

The teacher characteristics that we have identified so far appear to fit the teacher role rather well, minimizing strain. In some respects, however, these very characteristics are not quite suited to other aspects of the role and thus may be a source of strain. The strong orientation toward persons, especially the need to be liked, may well be a source of role strain at times. The teacher role requires him, like other group leaders, to demand task achievement at the expense of the pupil's socioemotional needs: this engenders hostility and dislike. To the extent that teachers meet antagonism

---

29. Davis, *op. cit.*

30. E. K. Strong, Jr., *Vocational Interests of Men and Women* (Stanford: Stanford University Press, 1943).

31. W. C. Tanner, Jr., "Personality Bases in Teacher Selection," *Phi Delta Kappan*, Vol. 35 (1954), pp. 271–77; MacLean, Gowan, and Gowan, *op. cit.*; C. J. Moore and D. Cole, "The Relation of MMPI Scores to Practice Teaching Ratings," *Journal of Educational Research*, Vol. 50 (1957), pp. 711–16.

32. J. C. Gowan, "Relation of the 'K' Scale of the MMPI to the Teaching Personality," *California Journal of Educational Research*, Vol. 6 (1955), pp. 208–12.

from less motivated or less capable pupils and their parents, they are apt to be distressed.

Another rather distinctive characteristic of seniors planning to enter teaching is their response to the item in the Davis survey "making a lot of money." [33] Only 12 percent checked this item as important, compared with almost 50 percent of the law and business seniors. Other studies have found that education students are near the bottom in ranking money and security as important; [34] male education students also rank lower than men in general on economic values. [35]

This characteristic fits one aspect of the role but may create strain with respect to another. The absence of ambitions to earn a great deal of money enables the teacher to tolerate relatively low pay; on the other hand, the low pay teachers receive may make it difficult for them to "keep up with the Joneses," a need consistent with their sensitivity to the opinions of others and their desire to be accepted by them.

PROCESSES THAT REDUCE ROLE STRAIN

In our attempt to gain an understanding of the role of the teacher, we have emphasized sources of strain, particularly those arising from social system and cultural elements. Such an analysis presents a rather dismal view of teachers as inadequately rewarded, overly frustrated, and subject to a variety of disparate and often conflicting and competing expectations that make it impossible for anyone adequately to fulfill this social role. Fortunately, this is an unrealistic picture. Many teachers do serve adequately, and with considerable personal satisfaction. In part, they are able to do this because of certain processes that operate to reduce role strain, processes that characterize the social system and individual behavior. We will examine these features in the context of a general social psychological theory of role performance.

Role Perception and Role Strain. Our examination of sources of conflicting role expectations has inevitably distorted the degree of strain that teachers experience, since we have not yet examined the

---

33. Davis, *op. cit.*
34. Rosenberg, *op. cit.*
35. MacLean, Gowan, and Gowan, *op. cit.*

role from the point of view of individual teachers. The distinction between actual and perceived role discrepancies should be kept in mind. Role partners may have discrepant role perceptions but be unaware of this. Or they may perceive discrepancies that actually do not exist. Discrepancies that partners are unaware of are likely to cause difficulties only if they lead to *actions* which frustrate the needs of one or both. Whether they exist or not, discrepancies that are perceived are sources of psychological discomfort. As social psychologists have long emphasized, it is our ideas about the world that influence us rather than objective reality. Studies of role perception suggest the operation of a number of principles which, for the most part, reduce the strains that we have previously discussed. We have already touched on one such principle. We noted in our discussion of role consensus the tendency for partners to see their role in a fashion that maximizes their outcomes. To the degree that teachers attribute such advantageous elements to the definitions others have of the teacher role, perceived role consensus is heightened with respect to these role elements.

This idea of defensive perception was evident in a comparison of the *beliefs* teachers had regarding their role, those which they attributed to school administrators, school board members, and parents, and the *expressed expectations* of these three groups of role partners.[36] In the relation of greatest significance to teachers, that involving their administrators, teachers perceived considerably more consensus than actually existed. They did, however, appear especially sensitive to two role demands. They felt more obligation to engage in community activities than was actually demanded by their role partners, and they perceived their role partners as restricting their role in the educational decision process to a greater extent than these partners did.

These findings and those of another study,[37] however, are subject to another interpretation. These respondents may have attributed a more restrictive and conservative definition of the teacher role to other persons than they held themselves. In a sense they were conveying to the interviewer the idea that other people make unreasonable demands on the teacher but that they did not do so themselves.

---

36. L. A. Doyle, "A Study of the Expectations Which Elementary Teachers, Administrators, School Board Members, and Parents Have of the Elementary Teachers' Roles," unpublished doctoral dissertation, Michigan State University, 1956.
37. Biddle, Rosencranz, and Rankin, *op. cit.*

This could be a product of a general tendency for respondents in an interview to give what they perceive to be the more socially desirable response.

A later study found that the reverse is true for teachers themselves. Unlike the other respondents, they attributed to other teachers more liberal definitions of the teacher's role than they themselves held.[38] Again, this might be interpreted as an attempt by the respondent to impress the investigator with the idea that he as a teacher held higher standards for the teacher role than other teachers. One can only speculate as to which is the appropriate interpretation. It could be that perceptual processes accentuate role conflict in these two areas, or it could be simply an artificial result of the methods employed.

The use of defensive perception to reduce role strain is clear in the findings on *occupational centrism*. Teachers, like other occupational groups, are accurate in assessing the relative prestige of occupations, except for their own, which they distort upward. This reduces the strain induced by the disparity between a favorable self concept and the perception that others view one less favorably.

Role Performance and the Resolution of Role Strain. Both the volume and disparity of role expectations facing most persons are such that it is impossible to meet all of them. As a result, partners bargain [39] or negotiate [40] to reach agreement on which expectations should be met. Perhaps the most commonplace example of this process occurs in the classroom, when the teacher tells his students at the beginning of the term what he expects of them and what he will do in return. In effect, he says, "If you children are orderly and diligent we will have lots of fun and accomplish a great deal." Typically, however, the pupils are not given an opportunity for an opening statement. They react generally by testing the limits of the proposed bargain: they try to obtain more in exchange for less. Out of this testing there gradually evolves an understanding of the degree to which each will fulfill the expectations of the other. The teacher, for instance, may tolerate a certain level of classroom noise at certain times; the students in turn may heed his expectations for a certain degree of diligence.

---

38. Green and Biddle, *op. cit.*

39. W. J. Goode, "A Theory of Role Strain," *American Sociological Review*, Vol. 25 (1960), pp. 483–96.

40. B. G. Glaser and A. L. Strauss, *Awareness of Dying* (Chicago: Aldine, 1965).

Similar bargains will be worked out with the principal, parents, school board members, janitors, and other role partners in the system. The character of these bargains, as reflected in the role performances of the persons involved, will be influenced by (1) congruency between the role demands and the values, needs, and abilities of the persons; (2) the role demands which each makes on the other; and (3) the degree to which each can and will impose effective sanctions for adequate role performance. These factors in turn are influenced by social and cultural variables.

We have already noted that, of his various role partners, it is the pupil who disagrees most with the teacher on his role. We suggested that the disparity was in part related to the emphasis the teacher places on his instrumental function as a leader in the learning process. Since this emphasis often interferes with the satisfaction of the pupils' socioemotional needs, conflict results. Class discipline is probably the greatest source of strain in his role. Fortunately, one social system feature eases this conflict: the unequal social power of the role partners. Students generally can exercise far fewer sanctions against the teacher than he can against them. An examination of the conditions under which there is maximum teacher-pupil conflict and consequent role strain for the teacher bears out the principle that conflict increases as the power of the pupil approaches that of the teacher. We have already applied another social psychological principle in explaining conflict between teacher and pupil. We noted that conflict increased to the degree that there existed a disparity between the teacher and the pupil in emphasis on instrumental achievement versus the satisfaction of socioemotional needs. This principle led us to expect maximum conflict in high school. This second principle makes a similar prediction. In high school the student is in many instances equal or superior to the teacher in sheer physical power. The teacher suffers a particular disadvantage in lower-class school districts, where such potential power on the part of a student is more likely to be actualized. Equality in physical power similarly holds true for the college group; however, among college students, who are primarily middle-class in orientation, physical prowess is ruled out as a potential source of power by strongly held norms against the use of physical violence. More than the elementary school child, the high school student is also able to hold his own in resisting certain sanctions practiced by the teacher, such as humor, sarcasm, or ridicule.

The power one person exercises over another depends not only on his ability to wield various sanctions but on characteristics of the other that make him susceptible to these sanctions. The teacher who is overly concerned with being liked by his students is subject to a powerful sanction, rejection. Here again, the social system operates to protect most teachers against this danger. Teachers, like other leaders, are generally protected from the development of strong emotional dependence on their followers by norms of social distance. Rules that require the student to behave in a respectful and distant manner toward the teacher or rules that prevent a teacher from dating his students reduce the chances that the teacher will develop strong emotional ties with a student. These norms of social distance governing the student-teacher relationship rather interestingly are enforced not only by the teacher but also by other partners—for somewhat different reasons. Other students may apply sanctions to a student who becomes too friendly with his teacher because such a relation is thought to give him an unfair competitive advantage over them in the grading process. Fellow teachers may apply sanctions against the teacher who goes out of his way to form close relationships with students. This norm functions to protect teachers from unfair practices used by other teachers to gain the student's esteem. Finally, parents and other community members may also favor the norm of social distance, particularly as it applies to cross-sex relations between teacher and student, as a protection for the student against possible sexual exploitation by the older, more powerful teacher.

The social power that position occupants wield over role partners depends not only on the sanctions each holds and their susceptibility to the sanctions of others but also on the potential coalitions which each can form with others. The teacher's power over the pupil may be reduced to the degree that the pupil can obtain aid from other role partners in the system, particularly the principal and the parent. Studies of the teacher in the authority structure of the school agree in concluding that the teacher's power is greatly influenced by the degree to which the principal can and will back him up.[41] To the degree that the principal forms a coalition with him rather than with the parent or student, the teach-

---

41. Gordon, "The Role of the Teacher in the Social Structure of the High School"; H. S. Becker, "The Teacher in the Authority System of the Public School," *Journal of Educational Sociology*, Vol. 27 (1953), pp. 128–41.

er's power is enhanced. The power of the parent in support of the pupil in middle- and upper-class districts may augment the pupil's power, increasing the strain felt by the teacher in these districts because of the extent to which he feels he must honor the students' expectations in the performance of his role.[42] Fortunately for the teacher, the structure of expectations that make up the teacher-principal relation generally includes the expectation that the principal should back up the teacher in any conflict with pupils or their parents. In summary, the amount of strain the teacher experiences in his relation with students, the manner in which he portrays his role, and the bargain that he and his pupils strike will depend in part upon their relative power.

One feature of social systems that relieves role strain is the physical and temporal separation of roles involving conflicting expectations. Under the conditions of small-town life, which characterized much of America until relatively recent times, this feature was not present. The teacher could be observed by all in a variety of settings, at work as well as at play. But under conditions of contemporary urban living this separation of his roles does help to relieve strain. The teacher role can be confined largely to the classroom setting. After hours he can function in a variety of conflicting roles as a citizen, as a participant in a variety of recreational pursuits, and so on without being under the surveillance of persons likely to judge his conduct as inappropriate for a teacher. It is this emerging feature of modern urban living that has greatly reduced the restrictiveness of the teacher role in American society.

Frequently social systems have features which protect members particularly vulnerable to conflicting expectations from sanctions. The lawyer, for instance, is accorded the right not to divulge any information prejudicial to his client. One feature of the school system appears to have this function. We refer to the normative expectations that ensure the privacy of the classroom. Teachers normally do not enter another teacher's classroom without permission; [43] visits by principals and others are generally carried out only on the basis of some understanding with the teacher. Similarly a variety of norms in the system have the effect of protecting the teacher from sanctions from pupils, parents, and other persons out-

---

42. Becker, *op. cit.*
43. Becker, *op. cit.*

side the school system. The norm generally observed by teachers never to criticize another teacher in front of students, parents, or other community members is such a protective norm. Tenure regulations in many elementary and secondary schools and in most colleges and universities are another case in point. They function to protect the teacher in the exercise of his role against the sanction of dismissal.

So far our discussion may have suggested that all of the various conflicting and competing expectations have equal priorities. This is rarely the case. One feature of social systems which helps individuals resolve the dilemma of conflicting expectations is the emergence of a set of priorities governing which expectation takes precedence in a given situation. These priorities are called *role hierarchies.* Thus in a university the expectation that a professor meet his classes has a higher priority than the expectation that he attend committee meetings. Should the time of a meeting coincide with one of his scheduled classes, his fellow committee members would acknowledge the precedence of his obligation to his class. At the same time, attendance at professional meetings in most instances takes precedence over meeting one's classes. The instructor who attends the national or regional meetings of a professional organization is generally free to dismiss his classes for the duration of these meetings, although he may arrange for substitute activities on their part during his absence, such as reading assignments or examinations.

Cultural Variables, Role Strain, and Role Performance. A number of cultural elements help to reduce role strain. The ideology of academic freedom, as our previous comments suggest, safeguards teachers and provides them with greater leeway in the performance of their role. The ideology of professionalism has the same effect. To the degree that his role partners see the teacher as a professionally trained person they are likely to accord him greater latitude in defining his role. Further, to the degree that his profession supports a particular teaching-learning ideology, he is apt to experience less role strain. His role expectations therefore have greater clarity.

Finally, whether a teacher believes in the tenets of progressive education or is more traditionally oriented should affect the manner in which he plays the role of leader in the educational process. Unfortunately, this last variable is often confounded with variables at the individual level, to which we now turn.

Individual Variables and Role Performance. A person's needs, values, abilities, and personal or physical attributes such as age will facilitate or hinder meeting a given role expectation. In an earlier section we noted that this affects the selection and retention of a role. To the degree that a person's attributes facilitate role performance he is likely to select that role and remain in it. This same principle sheds light on how he plays his role, which expectations he will meet or avoid. Peterson's study of interaction between the teacher role and the age and sex roles illustrates this principle: teachers of different ages were found to differ in styles of teaching.[44] In part this may reflect differences in the prevailing ideology associated with the period in which the teacher was trained. The younger teacher more frequently embraces the progressive as opposed to the traditional approach. Yet the reminiscences of older teachers regarding their early days of teaching bear out the observation that, in comparison with older persons, young persons find certain ways of relating to students more rewarding than other ways, irrespective of, or in addition to, ideological differences.

Peterson noted that the youngest teachers enacted their role as group leaders who were not much different from their students. The middle-aged teachers adopted a role that was less equalitarian, much like the parental role. It seems likely that the young teachers' style of leadership reflected the fact that, given their age, they could play that role with effectiveness. As near-peers of the students they could wield influence in the training process through referent power,[45] which rests on the followers' identification with the leader. Identification in turn is fostered in this context by the near similarity in age. When identification leads to the internalization of the leaders' goals, in this instance the teachers' goal of academic accomplishment, the task of the leader is greatly eased. Probably this role is also most congenial to the needs and interests of

---

44. W. A. Peterson, "Career Phases and Inter-Age Relationships. The female High School Teacher in Kansas City," unpublished doctoral dissertation, University of Chicago, 1956; Secord and Backman, *Social Psychology.*

45. J. R. P. French, Jr., and B. H. Raven, "The Bases of Social Power," in Dorwin Cartwright, ed., *Studies in Social Power* (Ann Arbor: University of Michigan Press, 1959), pp. 118–49.

the young teacher. In many ways it is like the role of the successful adolescent leader, a role that the teacher may well have aspired to in his relatively recent past. With increasing age, however, the teacher is forced to change his role portrayal. Peterson comments:

> The evidence is considerable that, beginning in the thirties, there is a decline in intimacy with the students. Some older teachers by virtue of a keen sustained interest in their subject matter, accompanied by an established prestige, seem able to maintain effective, though not especially intimate, relationships with students.[46]

The fact that the teachers described their early years of teaching as considerably more satisfying than the later ones suggests that the former role is more congenial to the needs of the typical teacher. Certainly the strong need to be liked would be more frequently satisfied in the more intimate role of the young teacher.

Although there has been little study of this, we suspect that the latitude that exists in the teacher role permits many other types of role enactment suited to the individual personality of the teacher. Those who are rather poorly suited to teaching may nevertheless remain in the educational system. Some, for example, may take administrative posts more suited to their personality and temperament, and others who desire a closer, more intimate relation with students may become counselors. But even those who remain in the classroom may portray their role in a style relatively well suited to their personality and in a manner that produces relatively effective teaching. All of us have been students and can recall the very different approaches taken by our own teachers, each effective in its own manner. Some make liberal use of jokes to liven up an otherwise dull presentation or discussion. Others, through their own enthusiasm, are capable of making a subject exciting to at least some students. Still others succeed through the extensive use of classroom projects which take advantage of group processes favorable to learning.

Implications for the Classroom

In drawing implications for the classroom, we will assume that excessive role strain reduces the teacher's satisfaction in his work and interferes with his effectiveness. This assumption

---

46. Peterson, *op. cit.*, p. 232.

is logical, although little evidence is available to support or refute it.

One source of role strain comes from disagreements on teaching practices that the teachers may have with school officials and parents. Factors that would increase the professional status of the teacher would probably relieve some of this strain—administrators and parents would be more inclined to defer to his judgment in classroom activities. The frequently made recommendation that a category of master teachers be created, through special selection and training, would be one way of placing public school teaching on a more professional level. Teachers not in this category would also acquire more professional status by undergoing on-the-job training, conducted largely by these master teachers. Creating a category of master teachers might also alleviate the role strain that arises from the fact that school administrators are so often recruited from the ranks of physical education majors and coaches, who are apt to have different views of education from those who have more training in the arts and sciences. This would relieve role strain in two ways: teaching policies and practices would be determined largely by the master teachers, and the master teachers themselves would provide a new source from which school administrators might be selected. Of further importance is the point that the master-teacher category might attract more males into public school teaching because of the better pay and higher status. Although the proportion of male teachers has been steadily rising over the past few decades, currently only about one in every seven teachers is male.

Having a larger number of male public school teachers would have other desirable effects upon the classroom, particularly for male students. Boys more readily identify with male teachers than with female teachers. This is especially true among lower-class or disadvantaged boys, who are becoming an increasing problem in public schools today. Moreover, many female teachers put up with low salaries and poor working conditions, since they are married or plan to get married, and their salary is only a secondary source of income. Since teaching is a lifework for many male teachers, they are more concerned about better salaries, more status, and better working conditions. Better working conditions would include relieving teachers of the many menial chores that now form part of their work load.

A major classroom problem for teachers concerns the task functions versus the socioemotional functions of their role. Organizing and managing classrooms so that there is a balance between these two kinds of activities is essential. Some recognition of the necessity for this is already present in a sociostructural feature of elementary schools. Here children remain in the same classroom most of the day and have the same teacher for most subjects. They engage in numerous projects that allow for some social interaction. In this way they come to form a psychegroup as well as a sociogroup, and have an opportunity to engage in socioemotional interaction.

The junior high school represents a transition period, with some recognition still given to the socioemotional function through the institution of the "home room." Children meet in their home room once or twice a day, and the home room members often act as a group in participating in the social functions of the school.

These examples are not intended to imply that classrooms where subjects are taught by a teacher who is a specialist are devoted purely to task activities. The competent public school teacher of English, mathematics, or other subjects develops a personal relation with his students and mixes in socioemotional activities as he teaches his subject matter. This often takes the form of humor or social discussion.

Finally, the ambivalence concerning education that is prevalent in our culture and which accounts for some of the teacher's problems should gradually become diminished as our technology continues to advance. The need for education and special training is becoming ever greater, and this long-run trend will ultimately raise the value of education and the status of teachers to a satisfactory level.

Index

Abilities, 17, 28–32, 45, 73; and anxiety, in academic performance, 38
Ability grouping, 80–82, 90
Academic culture, 53
Academic performance, 33–35, 64, 110; and ability grouping, 82; anxiety as factor in, 35–39; classroom implications of factors in, 45–47; effect of school setting on, 55, 77–80; influence of peer groups on, 62–63; and self concept, 40–44. *See also* Educational achievement
Achievement motivation, 33–35, 61, 90
Acquaintanceship, exchange theory and, 24
Affect structure, 93, 97, 100, 105, 108
Ainsworth, M., 39*n*
Alexander, C. N., Jr., 85*n*
Allensmith, W., 114*n*
Altman, E. R., 59*n*
American Indians, 74
Anastasi, Anne, 29–30
Anderson, K. E., 110*n*
Andrews, T. G., 38*n*
Antioch College, 52
Anxiety, in academic performance, 35–39; in competitive activity, 106; optimum level of, 46; and structured teaching methods, 114
Argyle, M., 20*n*
Arithmetic achievement, 37
Articulation: of cultural system, 130–31; of reward system, 129–30; of social system, 127–29
Astin, A. W., 49*n*, 60*n*
Athletic prowess, 64, 107
Atkinson, J. W., 33*n*
Attitudes, 17, 28, 32, 68, 73; distinguished from social motives, 4
Ausubel, D. P., and Ausubel, P., 76*n*

Backman, C. W., 13*n*, 15*n*, 41*n*, 43*n*, 69*n*, 118*n*, 124*n*, 132*n*, 142*n*

Bales, R. F., 99*n*
Bandura, Albert, 110*n*
Barber, K., 100*n*
Barker, R. G., 58*n*
Battle, E. S., 76*n*
Bauerfeind, R. H., 59*n*
Becker, H. S., 11*n*, 102*n*, 107*n*, 139*n*, 140*n*
Behavior patterns, 3; group values and, 3; persistence of, 12. *See also* Norms
Behavior roles, 101
Bell, R. R., 12*n*
Bendig, A. W., 39*n*
Bernstein, Basil, 23*n*, 24*n*
Bible, B. L., 119*n*
Biddle, B. J., 119*n*, 120*n*, 136*n*, 137*n*
Biggs, J. B., 40*n*
Blau, P., 109*n*
Bledsoe, J. C., 42*n*
Bloom, B. S., 7*n*
Bloomfield, J. M., 22*n*
Blumenfeld, W. S., 59*n*
Bonney, M. E., 96*n*, 97*n*
Borg, W. R., 81*n*, 82*n*
Borgatta, E. F., 99*n*
Boyle, R. P., 57*n*, 61*n*
Boys: anxiety reported by, 37; educational goal values of, 62–63; self-esteem and academic performance of, 42, 43
Broadbent, D. E., 39*n*
Brookover, W. B., 11*n*, 43*n*, 117*n*, 122*n*
Broom, L., 84*n*
Brown, B., 22*n*
Butcher, H. J., 39*n*
Butterworth, C. E., 85*n*

Campbell, E. Q., 9*n*, 61*n*, 71*n*, 74*n*, 75*n*, 76*n*, 77*n*, 78*n*, 85*n*
Campbell, P. S., 58*n*
Capacity, prediction of, 29

147

A
B
C
D
E
F
G
H
I
J